THE TRADITIONAL HOUSEHOLD HANDBOOK

Alex Goffey

Contents

Introduction

It was my dream job. I had bought a smart summer suit, mugged up on the ins and outs of the magazine world and caught the train down to London to stay with my grandparents the evening before. This was to make doubly sure I was fresh and on time for the interview.

I was nervous, of course, but as grandma waved me off the next morning, I had a feeling the job was mine for the taking. And that is when it happened.

I didn't actually see the bird, but judging by the mess it made – all down the shoulder and front of my new suit – it must have been a big one. I was distraught. I turned to grandma with tears in my eyes.

She was admirable and always so resourceful, never seemed to panic and that day four years ago was no different. She took my jacket, went into the kitchen and came back with a pot of tea and a bottle of white distilled vinegar. She dried the poop with a hair-dryer and sponged the mess with a weak solution of the vinegar and water. By the time we had finished the tea, my suit was pristine.

I laugh now when people claim good luck if a bird does its business on you, because I say my good fortune that day was in having such a resourceful grandma. Not only did I get the job but it got me to thinking how in this 'disposable age' we have forgotten the traditional household tips and tricks that served the generations well through good times and bad, wartime rationing and economic depression.

Grandma kept her home spotless, her cooking couldn't be beaten and even in her 80s her complexion was that of someone 30 years younger. Grandad had the best garden for miles around and was able to fix just about anything with the bits and bobs he kept in the shed. Both lived well into their 90s with hardly any illness. It was all achieved on a budget without the over-the-counter medicines, branded cleaning products, ready-made meals, DIY and the garden centres we have today.

The more I talked to them the more I realised there was no need to spend good money on cleaning, beauty, gardening and DIY products. A few inexpensive bits and pieces from the kitchen cupboard and garden shed, mixed with a little knowledge and your house, garden, clothes and skin can look as good as anyone's at a fraction of the price.

I like to think the tips and tricks I have researched and collected over the last four years will be passed down to your own children and grandchildren. Try them out and fine-tune to your own needs, after all they have been tested and improved through the experience of past generations and there is no reason the process should stop now.

How Clean Is Your House?

KITCHEN

Of all the rooms in your house it's the kitchen that produces the most grease, hard to clean dirt and – not to put too fine a point on it – pong. Not to worry, the kitchen is also the place grandma found the weapons to fight back.

Baking soda, white distilled vinegar and salt make up the thrifty threesome both your grime and the makers of expensive cleaning products are afraid of.

Most often used to leaven bread and add lightness to cakes and biscuits, baking soda also has all the properties to make it a versatile kitchen cleaner. Its fine, crystalline structure gives it a gentle abrasive quality ideal for scouring surfaces. Being an alkali, it also helps cut through grease and neutralise organic odours.

Vinegar tastes great on chips but did you know its acidic nature makes vinegar a great disinfectant?

CLEANING YOUR COOKER

The Hobs

Spillages can clog the gas jets on your hob causing an erratic, spluttering flame. Remedy by placing them in a pan and boiling in a strong solution of baking soda. Quarter of a box of baking soda to half a litre of water should do the trick.

Glass-topped electric hobs can be a nightmare to clean but if you scrub with a paste of baking soda and water they will come up like new. You can add a little white distilled vinegar to the paste for extra sparkle.

The Oven

To help keep clean, sprinkle the oven floor with baking soda. It will help prevent spillages from baking on and neutralise odours.

We like to put it off but when the time comes to give your oven a deep clean, here's a time-honoured solution. Place a bowl of strong household ammonia on the top shelf and a bowl of water on the bottom. Leave in the oven overnight and the following morning remove the bowls, sprinkle the inside of the oven with baking soda, leave for a minute and then wipe off with a damp cloth or kitchen roll.

If you don't want to wait overnight then a faster fix is to apply a strong solution of baking soda and water to the oven walls and shelving, turn up the heat for 20 minutes and allow to cool down. Finish off by washing with soap and water.

Extractor Hoods

The fine mesh of the extractor above your hobs can become clogged with grease making it useless. Rinse a cloth in half a litre of hot water with three or four tablespoons of baking soda. Add a few drops of white distilled vinegar to the cloth and wipe your troubles away.

The Microwave

They're a fast and clean method of cooking but the odour of strong-smelling foods can linger inside even after washing with soap and water. Adopting an old-fashioned odour-eating method for these modern appliances seems to work.

Dissolve a couple of tablespoons of baking soda in a small microwave-safe bowl of water. Turn your microwave on full power and let the solution boil so its steam coats the inside of the oven, then wipe down using a damp cloth.

CLEANING YOUR FRIDGE

Lovely Outside

There's a tendency for white goods to yellow a little with age but if you follow this method your fridge will sparkle like new.

Dissolve half a cup of baking soda in four cups of water, sponge the solution over the fridge and leave it alone for 15 minutes. After you've had a cup of tea, come back and rinse the fridge. The yellow will come off with the baking soda. This method is good for all white kitchen appliances.

Lovely Inside Too

Place an open box of baking soda somewhere in the fridge. It will absorb smells and keep your fridge fresh for up to three months after which you should replace the box.

You should never cry over spilt milk but when a few drops go sour in your fridge the smell can make your eyes water. Now is the time to make up one cup of baking soda to half a litre of water and wipe the solution over the affected areas and neutralise the odour.

DISHWASHER

Hard water deposits can eventually clog your dishwasher and reduce its life expectancy. Vinegar can wash the problem away. Every couple of months, or more often if in regular use, place a plastic cup filled with white distilled vinegar in the bottom of your otherwise empty dishwasher. Run through the wash and rinse cycles but turn off and remove the cup before the drying cycle begins.

RUST MARKS

Rust marks on your appliances or on the floor where their feet touch the ground can be eliminated using a paste of baking soda and water and scrubbing. The gentle abrasive power is the key.

CLEANING YOUR POTS AND PANS

If your pots and pans have burnt on food and you want to clean them without using elbow grease then cover the base with an equal mix of water and white distilled vinegar. Bring it to the boil before removing from the heat and leaving overnight. Wash with hot, soapy water the next day.

Another method is to soak the pot in baking soda and water for a few minutes before washing.

To give pans a sparkle, try polishing with a cloth that has been rinsed with a mix of one part water to two parts white distilled vinegar.

NON-STICK PANS

Getting your non-stick frying pan clean without harming the coating can be a headache unless you utilise the fine, crystalline structure of baking soda. Mix up a paste of baking soda and water and scrub gently. Not only will it lift the grease without scouring but it will also get rid of any odour that clings to the non-stick coating.

CAST-IRON PANS

A heavy-based cast-iron pan is a boon in the kitchen but can become encrusted with food.

Make a paste out of cream of tartar and white distilled vinegar. Scour the pan using the mix and leave for half an hour or so before washing with soapy water.

GET YOUR CRYSTAL CLEAR

Use the juice from half a lemon to soak a clean cloth and use it to wipe away the stains.

SPONGES

Keep them smelling sweet with a spray of fabric odour remover.

You can also keep them fresh by sprinkling with baking soda and wetting them through.

ROASTING TRAYS

For an effervescent solution, sprinkle a generous layer of baking soda over the tray then pour a solution of three parts water to one part white distilled vinegar on top. A satisfying fizz will lift the grease right off.

CHOPPING BOARDS

Chopping boards can be a breeding ground for bacteria and the smell of food like garlic or onion can linger. Use a fizzy method similar to that for cleaning roasting trays and you can keep them fresh, clean and safe. Sprinkle with baking soda and then pour the white distilled vinegar over the top. Listen to the fizz and then rinse.

IVORY HANDLES

The handles on knives and forks can become discoloured with age. To prevent this, try rubbing the ivory parts with lemon juice.

BREAD BINS

Wipe the inside of your bread bin using a clean cloth dipped in white distilled vinegar. This will help prevent the formation of mildew and will make your bread last longer before it starts to become mouldy.

CHINA, TEAPOTS AND CUPS

The glazing on china can become scratched by cutlery over time. Rub toothpaste over the marks and leave it alone for a while to work its magic. Wash with soap and water to finish off.

I've been drinking my tea without milk for the last few years which helps save the pennies and to my mind improves the flavour. The only problem is the tannin leaves dark brown stains in the cup unless you wash straight away. To get rid of these stains make up a thick paste of baking soda and water. Rub it into the cup and leave it for a couple of minutes before wiping away.

If you can't get your hand into the teapot then fill the pot with two tablespoons of baking soda, a quarter cup of white distilled vinegar and top up with boiling water. Leave it for 20 minutes and then rinse clean for dazzling results. Rinse well before you make your next brew.

CROCKERY

If you've left the washing-up until the day after the night before, then adding a tablespoon of baking soda to the washing-up water will increase the power of your normal washing-up liquid.

RUBBER GLOVES

If you use rubber gloves to do the washing-up and you have long fingernails, then you are probably familiar with the problem of 'wet finger'. To prevent your nails puncturing the glove and reducing its lifetime, all you need to do is turn it inside out and fix sticking plasters or a little masking tape into the end of each finger.

STAINLESS STEEL

An old-fashioned response to dull stainless steel surfaces is to polish using screwed up newspaper.

CHROME FIXTURES AND FITTINGS

If you're in the habit of using fabric softener sheets in your laundry, you can use them again to polish your taps and other chrome-plated fixtures. They'll shine up a treat.

When you've finished squeezing the juice from a lemon don't throw the remainder away until you've used it on your chrome fixtures. Simply rub with what's left of the fruit for a lemon fresh gleam. Rinse with water and dry with a soft cloth.

To get rid of the rust on chrome-plate you will need to rub it with a scrunched up piece of kitchen foil.

YOUR KETTLE

When your kettle becomes furred with limescale it becomes less efficient and takes more energy to boil. Using filtered water prevents the build-up but the acid in white distilled vinegar can remove deposits already in place. Fill the kettle half-and-half with the vinegar and water and then boil before leaving overnight. Make sure you boil fresh water in your kettle several times before you use it again.

RUBBISH BINS

You can keep your bin smelling fresh by sprinkling baking soda in the bottom every time you replace a bin liner.

BATHROOM

With a little common sense and some tweaking, many of the tips you would use for cleaning in the bathroom can be used in the kitchen and vice versa.

In the Shower

It doesn't take long for mildew to form in the folds of your shower curtains if you don't wash them regularly. Use one part chlorine bleach to four parts warm, soapy water when you wash them and this will help keep the unsightly stains from forming.

Spraying your shower curtains with a white distilled vinegar and water mix will remove mildew.

For glass shower doors fill a misting spray bottle, which you can buy from a garden centre, with white distilled vinegar and spray the doors. Leave for a couple of minutes and then wipe it away with a sponge sprinkled with baking soda. Rinse the doors with water and dry to finish.

If your shower head is becoming clogged, unscrew it and boil in a half-and-half solution of white distilled vinegar and water for several minutes. If it won't unscrew or is made of plastic, try a different approach. Half fill a plastic bag with 100 per cent white distilled vinegar and place the shower head into the bag so it's covered by the liquid. Fix the bag to the shower head handle with an elastic band and leave it overnight. The next morning, rinse it clean.

Tiles

Mildew loves to sprout on the rough-textured grout between tiles. Use an old toothbrush or nail-brush to scrub it away with a paste of baking soda and water. If the mildew is really bad then use neat hydrogen peroxide to soften the grime and remove with a single wipe.

In the Bath

Add a couple of shakes of baking soda to your bathwater. Not only will it prevent a tidemark forming at the water-line but it will also soften the water which means your soap will go further.

Cut up an old net curtain and use the scraps to clean the bath. The material is mildly abrasive but will not scratch the bath.

Air Freshener

Punch a few holes in the top of a box of baking soda and place near the toilet. This will help absorb any unpleasant smells. If you add a little bath salt the air will be even more fragrant.

Toilet Bowl

Believe it or not, pouring a bottle of coke down the toilet and leaving it overnight will remove stains and make the bowl sparkle.

If you live in a hard water area then limescale can build up in the toilet bowl. First, you need to remove the water from the bowl. You can do this either by bailing or by using a plunger to push the water around the U-bend. Make up a half-and-half mixture of domestic borax and white distilled vinegar. Spread the mixture over the limescale and leave for two to three hours before attacking with a stiff brush. You can also use this mixture to remove deposits from around taps and other fixtures.

Lino Floors

You can get rid of scuff marks from shoes on linoleum floors by spraying with your regular hairspray and then wiping with a damp cloth.

Car touch-up paint is a tough, long-lasting solution for hiding burns and scratches on lino. You just need to find the appropriate, matching colour.

LIVING AND SLEEPING AREAS

Most of us spend the majority of our time around the house in our living rooms and bedrooms. In this section, you'll find some top tips on cleaning the drips and stains of everyday living and all you need to know about the annual spring-clean.

For further information on stains, have a look at the Washday Wonders chapter. Many of the tips can be adapted for soft furnishings and carpets.

Mirrors, Windows and Glass

Cold tea makes a great cleaner for mirrors. Alternatively, you could try adding some white distilled vinegar to water and using this solution to cut through greasy handprints.

For a quick and dry clean, a screwed up piece of newspaper is just the right texture for the job. This works for other glass surfaces too.

If a decorating mishap leaves paint on your windows or mirrors, try applying hot vinegar. This will soften the offending marks, making them easy to wipe off.

Paintwork

Baking soda on a damp cloth will remove crayon, pencil and even marker pen from painted doors and skirting boards. Rub gently.

Add half a cup of baking soda and an equal amount of white distilled vinegar to a litre of warm water for a general cleaner for painted woodwork. Use a sponge to wash the solution over the area to be cleaned and allow a minute or so for the magic to work. If the woodwork is greasy, try adding a cup of ammonia to the mix. Don't forget to try this method on an out-of-the-way patch first as it may not be suitable for all wood finishes.

Carpets

You should always remove larger articles of rubbish with a dustpan and brush, as occasionally your vacuum cleaner will suck a larger article up which can clog its hose.

If this happens then you can use an off-cut of garden hose to clear the obstruction. Just unplug the cleaner and remove its hose. The garden hose will be flexible and strong enough to poke through the cleaner's tube and remove the problem.

To make a home-made carpet shampoo you will need to reach for the white distilled vinegar again. Add one cup to five litres of water for the correct strength and clean using a soft brush. Remember to use the closet test first: find an out-of-the-way area of carpet, preferably one inside a closet, and test the shampoo to make sure the colours in your carpet are fast.

If you have a cat or dog, you'll know their hair can get trodden into your carpets. Use a piece of damp foam rubber to get rid of them – the hairs, not your pet!

The unsightly impact of a small burn on your carpet, caused by a cigarette or spark from an open fire, can be reduced by rubbing with the cut surface of a raw onion. If this doesn't work then clip away the burned bit with a pair of nail scissors and replace with a few fibres cut from an out-of-the-way spot. Glue them in place.

Fresh red wine stains can be treated by pouring white wine over the spillage. A second application may be needed before mopping with a cloth.

If you use bleach to clean vomit from carpets, it can end up smelling of bleach and vomit. Instead, remove as much of the vomit as you can by scraping and then sprinkle plenty of baking soda over the top. Scrub with a stiff brush, working from outside to in to prevent spreading, and then rinse with a wet sponge. Soak up the worst of the moisture with absorbent paper towelling and then sprinkle again with baking soda. Leave it alone for an hour, or until it's dry and then vacuum it up.

You can dissolve chewing-gum that has been trodden into your carpet by pouring a little hot white distilled vinegar on the sticky spot and then scraping with a butter knife.

Wooden Floors

For a polished clean you will need to fill a spray bottle one quarter full of white distilled vinegar and then top it up with water. Spray the solution onto the floor and use a sponge or mop to wipe.

Annoying, squeaky floorboards can be silenced with a judicious sprinkle of talcum powder in the gaps and joints. Use unscented talc unless you want the smell around your house.

Curtains and Blinds

An old pair of velvet curtains can be brought back to life by giving them a good brush before hanging them in a steamy bathroom for an hour or so. After their 'sauna', let them dry by hanging in a warm area but not in direct sunlight.

If those chintz curtains are starting to look a little worse for wear, don't worry. Give them a good shake and then rub with a clean, damp cloth. Finish off by rubbing some stale breadcrumbs into the fabric. All you need to do now is remove the crumbs with a good, stiff brushing.

Get hold of some ammonia crystals and some hot, dry bran and you can dry-clean your dark-coloured chintz. Put the curtains in a clean bucket. Warm a cupful of the bran in a pan (or microwave) and add it to the bucket together with a teaspoon of the crystals. Cover the bucket and give it a good old shake. Give the fabric a brush down and hang it outside for half an hour or so.

Don't throw out those old net curtains. Their gently abrasive quality means they are ideal for cleaning the bath with. Just cut them to your favoured size.

An easy way to tackle dusty Venetian blinds is to dip your hand in some soapy water while wearing an old pair of fabric gloves and then run it along the slats.

Wallpaper

Revive your walls by wiping them gently with a clean duster

that's been dipped in oat bran. Dip regularly, as the particles that do the work will need replacing.

Grimy fingerprints can be erased with an ordinary pencil eraser.

Toothpaste has a mildly abrasive quality so is ideal for removing stains from your wallpaper.

You can get rid of greasy spots on your wallpaper so long as they are within reach of an iron. Cover the marks with blotting paper that has been folded double and press with the warm iron. Make sure you change the blotting paper regularly, otherwise you will end up transferring the greasy mark from one spot to another.

Anyone who has small kids in the house will love this next tip to remove crayon from wallpaper. Simply heat the 'art' with a hair-dryer and it will wipe away easily.

Furniture

To get rid of cigarette burn marks on wooden furniture, mix up a half-and-half paste of baking soda and distilled white vinegar. Rub the mixture into the burn with a clean cloth. Finally, use a pencil eraser to get rid of the mark. Some furniture polish may be needed to complete the job.

Small scratches on wooden furniture can be hidden by rubbing them with an appropriately coloured wax crayon.

White rings on wood, caused by wet glasses and cups, can be removed with a mixture of salt and cooking oil rubbed in gently with a cloth. You could also try mixing equal parts white distilled vinegar and olive oil. Rub with the grain and polish for the best results. Don't try these techniques on antique or valuable furniture which should be restored by a professional.

To prevent wicker furniture yellowing with age, wash with warm salt water.

Leather upholstery can be revived by rubbing milk into the hide a couple of times a year. Polish dry with a clean duster.

Upholstered furniture benefits from a shake and vac. Sprinkle baking soda over your soft furnishings, leave for a few minutes and then vacuum it up. The baking soda acts as a deodorant and brings the freshness back.

To clean light-coloured oak you will need to apply a solution of one teaspoon of household ammonia to one litre of water with a brush. After you have done this, wipe it dry with a clean cloth.

Washday Wonders

COLOUR TEST

To check whether a coloured item is likely to run in the wash, simply wet a corner and squeeze it in a white towel.

HARD WATER AND SOFT WATER

Hard water contains a greater level of mineral deposits than soft. You'll know if you have it because your kettle will become clogged with limescale. Another simple way to test your water hardness is to half fill a glass milk bottle and add a dozen drops of liquid washing detergent. Cover the top and give it a good shake. If you get a big head of foamy suds all the way to the top of the bottle your water is likely to be soft. With hard water you'll be left with a fairly flat covering of soap on the surface.

It's worth bearing your water type in mind when doing the laundry as detergent works less well in hard water. Use slightly more detergent in your machine if you live in a hard-water area and less if your water is soft.

SOAP SAVER

If you're running low on washing powder then add a quarter of a cup of baking soda to it. It will help keep your clothes smelling fresh too.

ZIP IT

Remember to close zippers and fasten bras before clothes go into the washer as these can catch and tear delicate items.

A STITCH IN TIME

It's best to repair any damaged clothing before washing as a small hole can become a big one during the rigours of the spin.

SMALLS

Put your underwear and other small items inside a pillowcase during the wash to beat those lost-sock blues and prevent tangling.

ALTOGETHER NOW

Wash towels and other 'linty' items together and never wash with corduroy unless you like the speckled look.

PILLOW TALK

For a refreshing night's sleep you need to refresh your pillows. To plump them up and bring the fluffiness back, wash them in a large washing machine without any soap. Keep the pillow in its case and wash on a warm water, gentle setting. Run it through the spin cycle twice and then tumble-dry. Keep the dryer on a cool setting. To keep the feathers from sticking together, make sure you give the pillow a gentle shake every ten minutes or so. All pillows can be refreshed by placing in a tumble-dryer for a few minutes, even if they are not wet in the first place.

THE VALUE OF VINEGAR

It's great for pretreating stains, it's a fabric conditioner and it boosts your regular washing powder – white distilled vinegar can be a massive boon on washday so long as you're sensible. Make sure you test it first on a small, out-of-sight area as it can cause some dyes to discolour. Here are some of its uses:

- **Soap Residue.** If you're a little heavy on the washing powder, your clothes and sheets can come out of the wash covered with patches of white soap residue. You can prevent this happening by adding a cup or two of white distilled vinegar to the final rinse cycle.
- **Static Stopper.** A cup of white distilled vinegar in the wash will also prevent lint clinging to your clothes and will reduce static cling when it comes to wearing.
- **Wash It Whiter.** Wool, cotton and silk can yellow with age, so if you're hand-washing, add about half a cup of white distilled vinegar to the bowl. It will keep your whites, bright. Another way to banish the headache of dull whites is to chuck a soluble aspirin into the wash.
- **Soft and Fluffy Blankets.** Wool and cotton blankets will come out more softer and fluffier if you add white distilled vinegar to the final rinse.
- **Smoky Smells.** The smell of smoke from cigarettes or an outdoor fire clings to clothing. Hang them over your bath and fill it with hot, steamy water and add a mug of white distilled vinegar to bring the freshness back.
- **Protect Your Machine.** If you live in an area with hard water then white distilled vinegar can help slow the build-up of limescale deposits in your machine, remove soap residue and extend the washer's lifetime. Add a cupful to an empty wash cycle once every two months and let it run all the way through.

REDUCE THE PAIN OF STAINS

Stains have launched a thousand products but grandma's kitchen-cupboard remedies still play a role for the canny cleaner at a fraction of the price. With a little common sense you can adapt some of these for use on soft furnishings.

Make a Stain Remover

There's no need to spend pounds on stain removal products when you can mix one yourself. You'll need the following ingredients: Half a cup of baking soda, half a cup of ammonia, half a cup of white distilled vinegar and a squirt of liquid soap.

Put the ingredients into one of those misting spray bottles they sell in garden centres, hardware stores and pound shops and fill to the top with water. Give it a good shake. Spray the solution over any spots and stains before you wash in the normal way. The mixture will keep for ages in your cupboard, ready for action.

Freeze It!

The longer you leave a stain the more likely it is to become permanent. If you can't treat it straight away then put the article of clothing in a plastic bag and pop it in your freezer – it will keep until you are ready for the job.

Grass Stains

Grass stains can be encouraged out of your clothes by soaking in full-strength white distilled vinegar for half an hour before washing. Another method is to squeeze some white toothpaste onto the stain and scrub with an old toothbrush.

Yet another way to remove stubborn grass stains is to add three drops of household ammonia to a teaspoon of hydrogen peroxide (six per cent strength). Use a clean cloth to rub the solution into the stain. Make sure you rinse it out as soon as the stain disappears to prevent any bleaching of colours.

Bye Gum

Raw egg white is great for getting soft chewing-gum out of your clothes. Rub it over the gum and leave for a couple of minutes before working at it with your fingers.

Another method is to freeze the gum by putting the item in a freezer for a while. The gum becomes brittle and can be 'broken' off. For larger items that do not fit into your freezer, you simply rub an ice-cube over the gum to get the same effect. If there are any sticky spots remaining then soak them in white distilled vinegar for ten minutes or so.

Ink Spots

Ink can be difficult to remove. If you catch the stain when fresh and wet it's a good idea to cover it with salt which will soak some up. Repeat as necessary. On white clothing try rubbing with a cut lemon before applying the salt.

Spraying water-based blue ink with hairspray really works. Remove the sticky spray by dabbing at it with a cloth dipped in white distilled vinegar.

Ball-point pen marks can be rubbed away with white toothpaste. Leave it on for a few minutes before washing it off. Alternatively, make up a thick paste of baking soda and milk and rub it into the affected area. Give it a rinse and then wash normally.

Grease and Cooking Oil Marks

Grandma had a couple of tips for removing grease marks. Sprinkle talcum powder over a fresh mark and leave for several minutes before brushing off. Alternatively, place brown paper over the stain, on both sides if practical, and press with a hot iron. You'll find the grease transfers to the paper. (This is also the method to get rid of wax from material.)

You could also try rubbing a blob of shampoo into the affected area before washing as normal.

Scorch Marks

One way to remove a slight burn mark from white material is to cover the area affected with a clean cloth dampened with hydrogen peroxide. Place an additional dry cloth over the first and then press lightly with a warm iron. Repeat the process as necessary.

Bird Droppings

This is the one that started my fascination with traditional household tips after an unfortunate incident on my way to a job interview. First let the muck dry and then sponge it away with a mild solution of white distilled vinegar and water. Use a hair-dryer if you need to dry the muck quickly. Thanks, Grandma!

Grimy Shirt Collars

No matter how much you wash your neck in summer, shirts and blouses will often collect grimy rings on their collars and cuffs. Rub the ring with white chalk and leave it overnight before washing the next day. Alternatively, dampen the collar with warm water, sprinkle with cream of tartar and rub in. Then wash as usual.

Another option is to use shampoo on the offending collar, it's specially formulated to remove grease from hair and works on neck grime too.

Lipstick On Your Collar?

First smear a little Vaseline over the mark. Next, dab with hydrogen peroxide. Finally, wash as normal.

Beer Stains On Woollens

Hand-wash the item in lukewarm water to which you have added salt. When hand-washing woollens you should keep them completely submerged and supported by the water otherwise their weight may cause them to stretch. After washing in salt water, wash again as usual.

Beetroot Stains

These can be tough to remove, especially if dried in. First, rub in some washing-up liquid by hand. Dab the stain with a clean cloth which has had a few drops of ammonia sprinkled over it. Keep dabbing until the stain loosens and then rinse the garment in warm water.

Another method you can try, if the stain is fresh, is to stretch the item over the top of a bowl with the beetroot mark in the centre. Boil a kettle of water and pour it onto the stain from a height. It is best to do this in the bath to protect yourself from any splashes.

Blood Stains

If you catch them when fresh, blood stains are easy to remove by rinsing in cold water and washing afterwards in the normal way.

You can try the same method for dried-in blood, but if the stain clings stubbornly, try adding a few drops of ammonia to the water before washing as usual.

The method my grandma used was to wash in cold water with salt added. Again, make sure you wash as per the guidelines afterwards.

Chocolate Stains

So, the grandchildren have been around and left their sticky, chocolate pawprints all over your clothes. You will need to get hold of some glycerine and some biological washing-up liquid. Mix it into a solution and then blot it onto the stain using a clean cloth. Soak the fabric in neat biological detergent if any stain remains.

With white fabrics you can remove chocolate stains by dabbing with a cloth that has been dipped in bleach.

Tea and Coffee Stains

Add a tablespoon of borax or a couple of tablespoons of household ammonia to a sink full of warm water. Soak the offending item in the sink. This also works for cocoa spills and spots.

Newsprint

Some low-quality newsprint can leave you with inky fingers and if you're not careful this will end up over your clothes or furniture. To remove it, all you need to do is apply methylated spirit with a damp cloth.

Don't Sweat About Perspiration Stains

Soak the affected areas in a solution of one part ammonia to three parts water.

Red Wine

Try pouring white wine onto red wine stains. You can also cover the area with wet salt and leave it for an hour or so. You will see the stain leeching into the salt. After you've done this, wash the garment in the normal way.

Alternatively, soak it for a few hours in glycerine before washing as normal.

You can dab away small red wine stains on white materials using a half-and-half solution of six per cent hydrogen peroxide and water.

Rust Stains

For rust stains rub with lemon juice and salt and leave to dry in the sun. Be careful on materials which are not white as the interaction of sun and lemon juice can bleach the colour. To complete the treatment, just wash as normal.

Saucy Stains

Both tomato and brown sauce stains can be removed by soaking the affected garment in a mixture of water and liquid washing detergent. Scrape away any excess before you do this. When you've finished, wash in the normal way.

Underwear Stains

Difficult stains can be removed by soaking underwear in a bowl of lukewarm water with a small amount of hydrogen peroxide and liquid washing detergent. Rinse and wash using the usual method.

Mildewed Load

You should remove clothes from the washing machine as soon as possible after the wash is finished and start the drying process. If you leave them too long they can take on an unpleasant, mouldy or mildewed smell that can last for several washes.

If for some reason you do forget to unload, you will need to wash again. This time, add just a little ammonia to bring the freshness back.

Bleach Be Gone

Instead of bleach add half a cup of baking soda to liquid washing detergent. It will make your whites whiter and your colours brighter.

REVITALISE YOUR CLOTHES

Here are a couple of handy hints to keep your clothes in shape:
- A sticky zip can be made to run smoothly by lubricating its

THE TRADITIONAL HOUSEHOLD HANDBOOK

teeth with some pencil lead or candle wax.

- If the cuffs on your favourite top have lost their elasticity and hang loose around your wrists then try soaking them in hot water before drying with a hair-dryer. This is the one time when you want the fabric to shrink!
- Hang a small cloth bag filled with whole cloves in your closet. The odour will repel moths but the smell is sweeter to the human nose than mothballs.

IRONING

Some people claim to love ironing but for most of us it's a chore. I've collected a few hints and tips to make the whole thing quicker, more efficient and more effective.

Care For Your Iron

- The jets on steam irons can become clogged and inefficient, particularly if you live in a hard-water area. Use filtered water if possible. If using unfiltered tap water, then adding a tablespoon of ammonia will soften it and reduce clogging.
- If the jets are already clogged with deposits you can remove them by filling the iron with white distilled vinegar. Turn the dial to maximum steam and leave it steaming in an upright position for several minutes. Leave it to cool and then pour the water out. You will see the particles pour out as well.
- The base of your iron can become sticky and stained. Wipe marks away with a cloth dipped in white distilled vinegar.

Prepare Your Board

Place a sheet of aluminium foil underneath the cover of your ironing board. This will reflect heat back and cut the time it takes to press your clothes.

A wrinkle-free cover helps give wrinkle-free clothes. Try soaking the cover and fitting it to the board whilst it is still wet. As it dries, it should shrink to the shape of the board.

Pressing News

It's more efficient to iron your clothes when they are slightly damp. Do not iron soaking wet clothes however, as this may scorch the fabric.

Make sure your iron reaches the required pre-set temperature before you use it. This will prevent water from dripping onto your clothes and leaving a mark.

Get organised so that you start with garments that require low-temperature ironing and progress to those needing more heat, it's quicker and safer for your fabrics.

It's better to iron the double thickness sections of your clothes first. Start with the waistbands and hems on trousers and skirts and the collars, cuffs and shoulder areas of shirts.

Keep a damp sponge to hand. Dab it over any dry creases that form and then iron them away.

If you're ironing a pleated skirt, then attach clothes-pegs to the bottom of the pleats – it's much easier.

If you want a sharp crease down the front of your trousers, then turn them inside out and draw a line of wet soap where you want it. Turn them back the right way and iron in your crease. The soap will melt and then harden into a crease.

When you're ironing sleeves and you don't want a crease along them, a great tip is to use a rolled-up magazine. Cover it with a cloth and then place it inside the sleeve. The magazine will unroll slightly until it fills the sleeve.

Always iron silk on the 'wrong' side and when it's still damp.

Always turn corduroy inside out before ironing to protect the texture.

When ironing hems, seams and pockets, turn the article inside out. If you iron directly onto these features they can become marked.

Trousers and skirts can become shiny from wear and from ironing. Sponge the affected areas with a solution made from one pint of water with a teaspoon of ammonia added. Make sure you iron gently.

Spray your clothes with a solution of one part white distilled vinegar to two parts of water. This will prevent a hot iron from giving them an unwanted sheen. The golden rule, however, is not to press too hard and don't have the iron too hot.

In an emergency you can hang your clothes in the bathroom while you take a hot, steamy bath. The worst of the creases will fall out.

If you wear clothes straight from the ironing board they are going to crease quickly. You should avoid wearing or packing away for a few hours if possible, so get yourself organised and iron those work shirts the night before.

HOW TO FOLD AND STORE YOUR CLOTHES

There's no point spending precious time ironing only for your clothes to get creased in the closet. Here are a few tips, some from grandma and others from professionals.

Dress Shirts

It's good to hang a shirt but if cupboard space is limited then here is the alternative. Some claim it leaves even fewer creases than hanging.

- Button the shirt and lay it face down on a flat surface.
- Fold each sleeve horizontally so they are parallel to the shoulders and one is laid over the other.
- Next take hold of the seam at the bottom and the shoulder at the top and fold in vertically. Repeat on the other side. If you have done it right then you should have formed a shallow V-shape underneath the collar.
- Now bring the bottom of the shirt up to the shoulders.

Ties

Fold them in half and then roll them starting from the narrow end. Store them on their sides all together in a box or drawer.

Sweaters

Never hang a jumper as this can cause it to stretch and become misshapen. Instead, lay it face down with the arms spread. Bring the left arm to touch the right hem and vice versa so that you have made a rectangle. Fold the top half over the bottom.

SOME SHOE CARE AND CLEANING TIPS

When the winter comes and the paths are gritted you will often find white salt stains remain on leather shoes that have become wet. One way to get rid of them is to add a tablespoon of white distilled vinegar to a cup of water and blot with a clean cloth. Rinse the shoes with cold water to finish.

Remember to let leather shoes dry naturally. Drying them near a radiator can make the leather brittle. To speed up the process remove any insoles and stuff the shoes with screwed up newspaper.

The amazing deodorising properties of baking soda can be put to good effect in training shoes. Sprinkle some inside to maintain freshness.

You shouldn't use water to clean suede shoes as it can destroy the texture. Use a soft pencil eraser to get the worst of any dirt off.

Hold suede shoes over a steaming kettle for a few moments then use an old toothbrush to raise their flattened nap.

When the ends of your laces become frayed and difficult to thread, try dipping them in nail polish.

While we're on the subject of shoes, a friend told me a great trick she uses when she's desperate to wear a pair that feel a little tight. Sprinkle the inside of the shoes with talcum powder. It will help to reduce friction between your feet and the leather. You could try this with baking soda too. It will also work as an odour eater.

SECTION 3

DIY

PAINTING AND DECORATING

I Love the Smell of Vanilla in the Morning

The smell of fresh oil-based paint permeates the house and can be really unpleasant if you have to live-in while decorating. Try stirring a few drops of vanilla essence in the paint pot to take the edge off the pong.

Remove the Pain of Paint on Panes

One of the trickiest painting jobs to tackle is a window frame, particularly one with several panes. It is so easy for your brush to stray onto the glass. Masking tape works but is fiddly. Instead, dip your finger in some Vaseline, or another brand of petroleum jelly and smear it over the glass next to the wood. Any mishaps will wipe away with ease. If a few spots still spatter the glass, then you can wipe them away with a cloth dipped in white distilled vinegar.

You can use these tips to paint around light fittings and doorknobs too. Alternatively, you can wrap a doorknob in kitchen foil while you paint around it.

No matter how hard you try you will probably leave a few spots of paint here and there. As with all stains you should act as soon as possible. Scrape away as much paint as you can. If you work towards the centre of the spot you will prevent it from spreading.

If you're using water-based paint, clean water should get rid of the spot. If not, soaking with liquid washing detergent will complete the process.

Oil-based paint is tougher to remove, so after scraping, sponge it with turpentine and then wash immediately with warm water.

Box It Off

It's always a good idea to line your floors with newspaper or an old sheet before painting, in case of any spillages. But to prevent them in the first place here's a great tip. Take a cereal box and cut a paint pot sized hole in one side. Place the can in the hole. Not only will the box catch any drips that run down the side of the pot but it is also an awful lot harder to knock the thing over.

Take a Break

If you're half way through your painting job and have to take a break there's no need to wash your brushes and rollers. Simply place their heads in a plastic bag and seal the bag around the handle with an elastic band. Alternatively, wrap the brush head in cling film. If you're stopping for the day you can put them in the freezer overnight or until you are ready to continue.

Catch It

Painting the ceiling can be a messy business. Wearing a hat makes sense. Also, wear a pair of washing-up gloves with the ends turned up. They will catch any drips that would otherwise end up going down your arm.

Another neat trick is to make a hole in a paper plate and push the handle through. You'll never get paint in your eyes again.

Two Step

So you've painted the stairs and now you can't get up them to go to the toilet. What a mistake! Next time paint every other step, leave them to dry before painting the rest.

Brush Tips and Care

Choose Your Weapon Wisely

The difference in price between a quality brush and a cheap one is minimal compared to the difference in the quality of the finish. It really does pay to get a good brush.

There are two major types of brush bristles to look out for: natural, made from hog or ox hair – the ox hair is softer – and synthetic, which is usually made from nylon or polyester.

Natural bristle brushes should not be used with water- or alcohol-based coatings as they will absorb the paint, becoming limp and almost impossible to use. They are, however, the traditional choice for oil-based paint and varnish as they provide a smooth finish.

Bristles should be longer than the brush is wide (unless the brush is very wide) and each one should taper so that the brush is less thick at the tip than at the heel when you look at it edge on. They should feel smooth and soft when you run them across the palm of your hand. When you bend them, they should spring back into position and they should be held tightly in place to the handle with a metal cuff to prevent shedding.

Look After It

Once you have a good brush it's time to look after it – it will last you years.

If you're using oil-based paint then prepare your natural bristle brushes by soaking them in linseed oil the night before. They'll last longer and will be easier to clean.

Before you start painting, use a hairbrush or comb to get rid of loose bristles from your brush. It will save you picking them off the walls later and ruining the finish.

If any bristles do come off and stick to the wall then use a pair of tweezers to remove them and smooth over the blemish with a stroke of the brush.

Remember to clean your brushes after use. After using oil-based paint, pour some turpentine into a strong plastic bag making sure it is hole-free. Place the head of the brush inside and grip the neck of the bag against the brush handle. You can use the fingers of your other hand to massage the bristles through the bag until the paint is removed. Use water for water-based paint.

Give your brushes a final wash in some hot water. Add a little fabric conditioner to keep the bristles nice and soft.

Hang them out to dry on a clothes line using a little sticky tape attached to the handle. This prevents the bristles from becoming broken and bent.

If you've neglected to clean your brushes from your previous job then you can still rescue them by soaking them in hot, white distilled vinegar and rinsing with soapy water.

How Much Paint Will You Need?

First, you need to work out the surface area that needs to be painted. Divide the wall into easy-to-measure sections. Multiply the height of each section by its width and add each total together. The handy guide below is the approximate amount of paint needed to apply one coat.

- One litre of all-purpose primer will cover 12 square metres.
- One litre of undercoat will cover 16 square metres.
- One litre of gloss will cover 14 square metres.
- One litre of non-drip gloss will cover 12 square metres.
- One litre of emulsion will cover 14 square metres.

Remember that embossed or woodchip wallpaper will require more paint. Allow about one third extra.

How To Store Leftover Paint

A layer of turpentine poured over the surface of leftover paint will prevent a skin forming over the top. Pour it off before you use the paint again.

Storing the pot upside down will also stop a skin forming. Just be careful the lid is firmly in place first.

Use a marker pen to draw a line on the pot to show the level of paint remaining. Now you won't have to prise the lid open to see how much is left.

If your paint goes lumpy in the pot you can strain it through a pair of old tights stretched over the top.

Wipe Yourself Down

Now you've finished the job you'll need to clean yourself up. Instead of using harsh turpentine to get oil-based paint off your skin, use some olive oil or another cooking oil. It's much better for your skin. Another tip to make paint easier to remove is to rub your hands with Vaseline or another brand of petroleum jelly before you begin to paint.

Wallpaper

If you fail to strip old paper before hanging the new you're asking for trouble. The moisture from the fresh wallpaper paste is likely to permeate the original and both sets will come off the wall. If you do decide to chance hanging new wallpaper over the old then cover any greasy spots or water-damaged areas with some clear nail varnish beforehand. This will help prevent the stain from reappearing on the new paper a few weeks on.

You can buy liquids and gels to help strip wallpaper. However, a good old-fashioned sponge and bucket of hot water and white distilled vinegar solution does the job. Use a sharp knife to score horizontal lines in the paper every ten inches or so, taking care not to mark the plaster underneath. This will allow the solution to soak behind the paper and work its magic.

Before you hang your wallpaper, paint a strip of wall at the top the same colour as the ceiling. No one will be able to tell if there's an uneven line or slight gap where the wall and ceiling meet.

If you're using patterned paper, make sure you start with a complete block of pattern at the ceiling end. It is less noticeable if the design is incomplete down by the skirting board.

Use a spirit level when hanging each strip. It will ensure the vertical lines are spot on.

Keep hold of a few scraps of leftover wallpaper to repair any tears or other damage which inevitably occurs over the following years. Tear rather than cut the patch to size as this will make the join far less noticeable.

ODD JOBS

Squeaky Floorboards

If you can't cross the room without your squeaky, creaky floorboards waking the household, then here's a simple trick you can use. Sprinkle the offending boards with talcum powder, making sure it puffs into all the gaps. It should lubricate the area where the board rubs against the joist and reduce the noise.

For a more professional job you need to locate the joists nearest to the squeak. Joists are the 'beams' that the boards are attached to. As they get older the joists can shrink slightly causing the boards to shift, rub and squeak. Joists are normally laid from the front to the back of your house. Once you have worked out where the board rubs against the joist, drill a screw that is one and a quarter inches long through the board and into the joist. Now you will be able to indulge in your midnight feasts without disturbing the rest of the household.

Stick-on Hooks

They're great for hanging your dressing gown on the bathroom door but the sticky pads that fix 'no-nail' hooks to surfaces can be a nightmare to remove. Warm some white distilled vinegar in a pan and use a sponge to soak it into the pad. A few minutes later it should be easy to remove. This method is good for getting rid of labels from glass, china and wood as well.

Fixing a Torn Blind

If your window blind has a tear in it, take it down and lay it on a table. Hold the tear together with your fingers and apply several coats of clear nail varnish.

Hanging Pictures

A collection of family portraits and well-chosen prints can really personalise your home, but unless you have a helper to direct around the room it can be difficult to work out where to place the hook. Here's a great tip to make your job much easier.

Lay the picture face down on a sheet of old newspaper, frame and all. Trace a line around the frame and cut out the shape. Now all you need to do is find some sticky tape and fasten the shape wherever you want to try it out. Now, you can take as long as you want and change your mind as many times as you like.

When you're happy with the positioning you can fasten the hooks to the wall through the newspaper which will tear away easily. If you use this method you will never be hurried along by a partner grumbling about tired arms and you won't end up with an unnecessarily holey wall.

Plastering Tips

To prevent lumps from forming when mixing plaster you should add the plaster dust to the water rather than water to the plaster dust.

You can buy yourself some time by adding a little white distilled vinegar to the plaster mix. It will slow down the hardening process.

Cracking Plaster

To prevent plaster from splitting or crumbling when you hang a picture, mark the spot with a sticky tape cross before you hammer the nail through. Another top tip is to heat the nail before hammering. Use a lighter or a match.

To fill small cracks and holes in plaster, mix together baking soda with some white children's glue. Press the mix into the gaps using a butter knife and sand smooth when dry.

If there's a larger hole to plug it's a good idea to pack it with small scrunched up balls of newspaper before applying the filler of your choice. If you do the job with filler alone it may take days to dry. Using paper means you use less filler as well.

Rotten Window Frames

Packing with paper balls is a good technique to use if you need to fill a rotting window frame. Make sure you remove all the rotten wood. Substitute the plaster filler with wood filler.

Linoleum and Vinyl Floor Coverings

Getting a true fit when laying lino around door frames can be difficult. Use plasticine or Blu-Tack to make an impression of the awkward bit and draw around it to make a template.

Lino can stretch with use so it is best to leave it loose for a few weeks before fixing it in place.

Vinyl floor coverings, on the other hand, have a tendency to shrink. Make sure you leave a little extra at the edges. After a few weeks it should have settled down. Now is the time to cut it to size.

Sometimes lino wants to curl up at the edges. Fill a hot-water bottle and lay it in place over the lino which should soften and encourage it to lie flat.

Creaking Hinges

Pencil lead is in fact graphite which is an excellent lubricant. Take a normal pencil and draw with it all over the moving parts of the hinge. Open and close the door a few times and repeat the process as necessary. You may need to file some graphite from the pencil tip and then gently blow it over the hinge in order to get adequate penetration.

Electricity Socket

If it's getting difficult to pull a plug from its socket, draw all over its prongs with a soft pencil. The graphite will lubricate the metal making the plug easy to slip in and out. Make sure you fully remove the plug before attempting this.

Sticky Locks

Graphite is a far better lubricant for locks than oil as oil can gum up the works and will attract dust and dirt. If you're finding it hard to turn a key in its lock it's time to draw on the power of your pencil again. Scribble all over your key and jiggle it around in the lock. Again, you may need to file some of the graphite from the tip and blow into the keyhole.

Broken Key

If your key breaks in the lock then don't panic and call the locksmith just yet. Try placing a dab of super glue on the broken off piece where the break occurred and hold it against the part that is left in the lock. After a few minutes the join should be strong enough to remove the key.

Sticky Drawers

If you're having trouble opening your cupboard drawers, try lubricating the runners by rubbing a candle over them. Once you've done this it should be a lot easier.

Protect Your Bath

If you're carrying out a job in the bathroom then it is always a good idea to line your bath and your sink with a blanket. It only takes one slip, and a tool or even a screw or a nail could chip your bath unless it is protected.

Screws

On some furniture, particularly MDF, the wood around the thread of screws can become worn so that the screw just pulls out. If this happens, paint nail varnish on the screw and twist it back in. When the varnish hardens, your problem will be fixed.

If you're having difficulty unscrewing a screw out then try heating it. Use a soldering iron or touch the head with a red hot poker. The heat will cause the screw to expand thus removing any caked-on paint and when it cools it will decrease in size and should come out easily. Give it a sharp clockwise turn with your screwdriver and immediately and abruptly turn it counter-clockwise.

You could also put a few drops of white distilled vinegar around the head of the screw if it is rusty and stubbornly refusing to come out. Leave it for a while so that the vinegar works its way around the threaded sections before attempting to remove it again.

If you know you will want to remove a screw from wood before you put it in then try rubbing it with a little Vaseline or other brand of petroleum jelly before using.

If you are trying to place a screw in an awkward position you may find it helpful to place a spot of Blu-Tack on its head to hold it to the screwdriver. Some screwdrivers are magnetised to achieve the same effect.

Rawlplugs

If you're halfway through a job and you run out of Rawlplugs for your screws then you can use three or four spent matches in their place. These will grip screws in the same way.

Saw Teeth

There is nothing more infuriating than getting halfway through a plank of wood and finding your saw begins to stick. Lubrication is the answer. I have found that rubbing the teeth with soap is the best solution.

Sandpaper

Your sandpaper will be more hardwearing and will last longer if you back it with masking tape before you use it.

Don't Lose Your (Broom) Head

If you spend as much time reattaching a loose head to your broom handle as you do sweeping with it then try this tip. Wrap electrical tape around the end of the broom handle for a tighter fit.

Ornaments

You can protect your furniture and wooden floors by cutting the appropriate shape from a cork tile and sticking it to the base of sculptures, pottery and other decorative items.

Sharpen Your Scissors

Get hold of some sandpaper and fold it in two with the rough side facing out. Cut it and the sandpaper will sharpen your scissors for you. It is best to cut at the edge of the sandpaper to avoid wastage.

Candles

A single candle from a birthday cake will last for hours if you sink it into the middle of a jar of Vaseline or other brand of petroleum jelly.

Solve Your Lightbulb Problem With a Spud

Have you ever had to remove the remains of a lightbulb from the socket after the glass has shattered? It's a potentially dangerous situation unless you can get your hands on a potato.

Tap away any remaining glass with a spoon and cut a large potato in half. Press the cut side of the spud into the socket and unscrew the rest of the bulb. You can use a piece of soap instead if you wish.

Clogged Drain

If the water in your kitchen sink takes an age to go down the plughole it's more than likely clogged with grease. Pour one cup of salt and one cup of baking soda down the plughole followed by a kettle full of boiling water. This should work well. To give it a boost you might try heating the U-bend under the sink with a hair-dryer first. This will help melt any solid fat deposits.

Keeping Cool is a Breeze with Sash Windows

Sash windows are beautifully designed to keep the air in your house circulating. Once upon a time everyone knew how to get the effect up and running but it has become a forgotten art and many sash-style windows are now painted shut.

If your room is stuffy, open the sash windows from both the bottom and the top. Hot air rises and will exit from the gap at the top. It will be replaced with cooler air from outside, which comes in through the gap at the bottom. The air in your room will circulate and be replenished.

If your sash windows are painted shut you can tackle the job yourself but be warned, you may need to work on your muscles first.

Break the seal with a putty knife, tapping lightly with a small hammer if necessary. You may need to repeat both inside and out. If the window still won't open you will need to remove excess paint from the tracks using a chisel. Next, fix some sandpaper around a block of wood that fits snugly into the track and sand until smooth. Try spraying the tracks with a silicon lubricant. Good luck.

Leaky Pipes

An ingenious temporary fix involves wrapping a leaky joint in a pipe with ordinary string. Leave the end of the string to dangle in a jug or bucket. The water will run down it and into the receptacle, buying you some time before the plumber arrives.

ENERGY EFFICIENCY

You don't have to be on a budget to want to increase energy efficiency in your home. Using less energy is also of vital importance to help save the planet.

Chimneys

You can use plastic foam insulation to block any old and unused chimneys in your house. This will prevent unnecessary draughts.

Hot Water Heaters

Make sure your hot water tank is well wrapped to prevent heat loss. You can buy special jackets for the tanks but you can also make your own insulation using blankets. Two or three layers will keep more heat in than one thick one.

When installing a water heater it is best situated in a warm area of the house. If it is in an unheated garage or a cold room then it will have to get over the ambient temperature before it can heat your water and will be a lot less efficient.

Fuel

If you are running a coal or wood burning heating system it is a good idea to plan ahead and buy your fuel during the summer months when it is cheaper.

It is also worth keeping your eyes open for skips. You will often find they are full of wood which could be used for heating your home. It is good practice to ask the person who has hired the skip if it is okay to remove any items.

Draughts

It is amazing how much heat escapes underneath your doors. You can make simple but effective draught excluders from a tube of material stuffed with old socks and tights or other odd bits of material that you may have to hand and then sew at both ends.

Hang curtains or drapes over your patio doors and windows in winter.

Think About Your Cupboards

If you leave your cupboard doors open then they will automatically fill with the heat that should by rights be keeping you toasty warm. Make sure all cupboard doors are closed to prevent heat escaping into them.

Radiators

Make sure you keep your radiators well-dusted as a layer of dust can block some of the heat from radiating into the room.

Another top tip with radiators is to paste a sheet of aluminium foil onto the wall behind them. Instead of escaping through the walls of your house the heat will instead be reflected back into your room.

Instead of pasting the aluminium foil directly to the wall behind the radiator you can instead glue it to a piece of board which you can then slot into place.

It is best not to hide your radiators behind a long curtain as most of the heat will disappear through the window rather than into the room where it is useful. Instead, buy curtains that are short enough to tuck behind the top of the radiator.

Windows

You can create your own double glazing during deepest winter. You will need to get hold of some plastic sheeting. All you need to do is measure up your windows and cut the sheets to size. Once you have done this, then you can fix the sheets to the inside of your windows using some masking tape. It may not be the prettiest look, but the layer of air trapped between the window glass and plastic sheet will insulate your room and save a surprising amount of money during a cold snap.

Drying Clothes

The most energy-efficient way to dry clothes is to harness the energy of the wind and the sun. Somehow clothes feel fresher when they've had the chance to dry and air outside. For those of us without a garden however, this is impossible. Added to that, the British weather is not always ideal for outside drying.

Tumble-dryers use a lot of energy to do the same job as a washing line. They are probably the most energy-thirsty appliance in your house and typically use between 3.5 to 4.5 kilowatts of electricity to dry a full load. That's roughly equivalent to burning a 100 watt lightbulb non-stop for about 35 hours.

If you do use one then any tips to reduce the running costs can save you pounds over a year.

It takes far less energy to spin water out of your clothes than it does to heat them out in a tumble-dryer. Therefore, you should always use your spin cycle before transferring to the tumble-dryer.

Never take an armful of clothes from your washing machine and dump it straight into the tumble-dryer. It may take a few moments more, but when you take your clothes out of the washer you should loosen them and place each item into the tumble-dryer separately. This will allow the warm air to circulate more effectively. Make sure that sleeves are not tangled together. Pay particular attention to socks which often ball up in the wash and take a lot more time to dry than if they are straightened out.

Try to dry similar clothes together as this will ensure they dry more evenly.

Always try and fit the maximum load into your tumble-dryer at any one time. It is more efficient to dry a big load in one go rather than doing two smaller loads.

You don't need to get all of the water out of your clothes before ironing. In fact, cotton clothes are much easier to iron when they are still slightly damp. Therefore, you should not wait until cotton is bone dry before removing.

Some tumble-dryers have a special setting which means they stop automatically when there is still a little dampness in the clothes. This is usually called the 'iron dry' setting. If yours has one then you should use it. When the 'iron dry' programme is finished you can remove the damp cotton items from the load and then continue drying the rest on a 'cupboard dry' setting.

Tumble-dryers take the air from the room in which they are

situated. Therefore, where you put the tumble-dryer impacts on how efficient it is. If you have it in a cold garage or other outbuilding for instance, it will take a lot more energy to heat the air to the extent it can begin the drying process.

These days you can buy a tumble-dryer with an automatic sensor which stops the machine when the clothes are dry.

SECTION 4

Cooking Corner

A PROFESSIONAL CHEF TALKS

Dean Leach has been working in professional kitchens for the last 23 years, the last ten as a head chef specialising in modern British cuisine.

I popped into Holborn in central London to visit him following a busy lunch service to see if he could give me the benefit of his experience.

"The first thing I learned was the importance of ingredients," he told me from the kitchen of The Ship Tavern where he has worked for the last two years. "I started in Italian restaurants and they were passionate about choosing the best seasonal produce.

"Mussels were on the menu only when they were in season and we only served asparagus during the English season, for two months between May and June.

"It isn't just that seasonal produce is more environmentally friendly and of better quality than food imported out of season. It's great quality and because there is plenty of it about when it's in season I've found you can design a menu much more cheaply if you use it."

As I spoke to Dean, it wasn't long before I became distracted by the lovely meaty smells coming from one of his ovens. He opened the door and showed me some beef bones browning off ready for the stockpot.

"A good stock makes all the difference," he said. "I'm just sealing the bones. I'll add them to a pot along with some roughly-chopped onions, celery and carrots – the key ingredients for any stock or casserole. When I use herbs I save the stalks and they go into the pot as well."

The ingredients are covered with water and allowed to bubble away on the stove until all the goodness and flavour is concentrated before the liquid is strained.

"When it's ready," he said, "we'll need to get rid of the excess fat. A good tip is to add a couple of ladles of cold water, ideally from the fridge. It will cool and harden the fat which has risen to the top and we'll be able to skim it off with a spoon."

It was a privilege to spend time in such a well-run kitchen with an experienced chef and I couldn't leave without asking for a couple of extra tips.

"You can buy balsamic syrup in the shops which is nice and thick and lovely in salad dressings, it really coats the salad whereas a thin balsamic vinegar won't.

"The only problem is it's expensive but if you want to make your own you can reduce balsamic vinegar in a pan. Just add some demerara sugar during the reduction. It will be nice and sweet and sticky.

"My personal style is Modern British. The key is using modern techniques in traditional recipes. When you're making a casserole the traditional way is to use roughly-cut stock vegetables that you can still see when the dish is served. That's fine and it still tastes great. For me though, I like to blend my celery and carrots. The sauce is richer and more velvety and it's what you would expect in a top restaurant."

MORE COOKING TIPS

Meat

The best way to freeze minced meat is to place it in a plastic bag and flatten it so it looks like a pancake. Not only will this minimise the space it takes up in your freezer but it will also help it thaw out much more quickly when the time comes for you to use it.

Do you ever have a problem with curled up edges when you fry or grill bacon? There's no need to cut into the fat to make it stay flat. Instead, dip it into some iced water for a few seconds and pat dry with a paper towel before cooking.

Rub a cut lemon over the skin of chicken before roasting. It will aid the crisping process.

To remove a layer of fat from stock or gravy, drop some ice-cubes into the pot. The fat will cool and harden against the ice-cubes. You can also remove excess fat by placing a few lettuce leaves in the pot.

It's easy to turn sausages under the grill, on a barbecue or in a frying pan if you thread them along a sharp skewer first.

If you are making a burger, the usual method used to bind it together is to use an egg. However, you can replace the egg with some grated Parmesan cheese. Not only will it hold the burger together well but it will add seasoning and richness.

After you have shaped your burger remember to leave it alone in the fridge for a while so that the flavours can mingle and the ingredients can get to know each other a little better.

If you are planning a barbecue then boil your sausages the evening before. It will keep them fresh, ensure they are cooked through and prevent them from splitting on the grill.

Boiled ham can be a little salty. Try adding some wine or cider vinegar to the water in which you boil the joint and it will help to draw out the salt as well as improve the taste. You could also add some apple slices to the water to draw out the salt.

Adding a little white distilled vinegar when boiling tough meat will help to make it tender.

Marinate beef in a dish containing some pineapple juice or failing that some white distilled vinegar. Leave it for several hours to tenderise. Just make sure you rinse the marinade away before cooking.

A square of dark, bitter chocolate added to a game, chicken or turkey casserole will help impart a lovely rich flavour.

Minced meat will go further if you add fresh bread crumbs or porridge oats. These ingredients will also thicken the sauce for you.

When making Scotch eggs mix fresh breadcrumbs with the sausage meat. It will go further and you probably won't notice any difference in flavour.

You can prevent the cut end of a ham from becoming mouldy if you rub some white distilled vinegar into it.

Fish

Add lemon to the fat when cooking fish. Not only does it add taste but it will make the pan easier to clean afterwards.

Thaw fish in milk to give the illusion that it's freshly caught.

Instead of using water to make a batter, replace it with beer to add extra flavour. Not only is it tasty but the bubbles in beer add air to the mix making the batter lovely and light.

When cooking any type of fish whole, a tasty tip is to slip a bay leaf inside. It really helps to bring out the flavour of the fish without dominating it.

You can remove fishy smells from your hands or worktops by rubbing with butter.

Coat your fish in flour, seasoned with salt and pepper, before shallow frying. Not only will it keep the fish from falling apart in the pan but it will also stop it from drying out during the cooking process.

Fruit and Vegetables

Mushrooms often come packaged in plastic but if you want them to last longer and not to go slimy and musty then you should transfer them to a breathable paper bag for storage. Keep them in the door of your fridge rather than in a colder part.

To reintroduce a fresh taste to frozen vegetables, pour boiling water over them as soon as they come out of the freezer.

Garlic tastes lovely and sweet when roasted. Place a whole bulb on a roasting tray in your oven with a little olive oil. Leave it for an hour on a medium heat. Squeeze the toffee-like insides out of each clove and mash them together in olive oil. Now you can spread the resulting mixture on toast as a healthier alternative to garlic butter.

Root vegetables, like carrots and parsnips, will keep fresh for longer if you cut off their tops before storing.

Reduce the cooking time for baked potatoes by placing a metal skewer all the way through when baking. The metal conducts the heat right into the middle of the spud. If you don't have any suitable skewers then a clean nail will do the job just as well.

If you only use half an onion in a recipe you can preserve the remainder by rubbing the cut side with a little butter.

For crispier and golden roast potatoes, boil them first in well-salted water. Bash them around in the pot before adding to the roasting dish. Alternatively you can score them with a fork.

To make your mashed potatoes more fluffy, add half a teaspoon of sugar to the water when boiling.

New potatoes are the taste of early summer. To make them easier to scrape try soaking them in cold water with a tablespoon of bicarbonate of soda added.

It's always a good idea to prepare your vegetables before you begin to cook. To prevent potatoes from becoming discoloured once they've been peeled just place them in a bowl of cold water to which a tablespoon of milk has been added.

Keep your cauliflower lovely and white by adding a teaspoon of white distilled vinegar to the cooking water.

You can make bacon-flavoured chips by adding a bit of bacon rind to the chip oil when frying.

Make an attractive and curly carrot side dish by slicing a large carrot with a potato peeler. Pierce one end with a skewer, twist the carrot strip and then pierce the other end. Squeeze several of these onto each skewer and store in cold water. Cook as usual and remove from the skewers when ready to serve.

Hold a teaspoon in your mouth to prevent your eyes from watering when slicing onions.

We are all familiar with the sulphurous smell of boiling cabbage which seems to get all around the house. I know one person who used to refuse to cook with this majestic vegetable as a result. That was until she heard this tip: Simply add a large sprig of parsley to the water before boiling.

Another method for reducing the pong from boiling cabbage is to add a little white distilled vinegar to the water.

If your bananas are getting past it there is no need to throw them away. Mashed-up over-ripe bananas will store in the freezer to become a ready-made flavouring for cake and biscuit mixes.

Salad

You can revive limp lettuce by placing it in a bowl of iced water for half an hour before using.

Don't keep celery in the plastic bag it came in. Store it in a brown paper bag instead, this will help it keep longer.

Tomatoes will ripen more quickly if you store them in a brown paper bag. This works with peaches, pears and avocados too. Make sure you arrange them in a single layer within the bag rather than stacked on top of each other.

To remove the skin from tomatoes put them in a bowl of boiling water for 30 seconds first. You can also hold them over the flame of your gas hob until the skin starts to split and pop.

If your tomatoes have become over-ripe you can bring them back by placing them in a pan or bowl and covering them with cold, salted water for an hour or so.

Green, unripened tomatoes can be used in chutney. If you want them for eating fresh however, you can speed up the ripening process by placing them in a bowl together with an already ripe tomato or an apple.

For a healthy alternative to the bun, try wrapping your burgers in a salad leaf instead. Lettuce is ideal. You can add mayonnaise and other condiments and the leaf will ensure everything is held in place.

Lovely, peppery watercress will last longer in your fridge if you store it head first in a bowl of water.

Baking

You can make baking powder by sieving together one part baking soda, one part cornflour and two parts cream of tartar. Make sure the ingredients are properly mixed.

Plump up dried raisins by placing them in hot water for a few minutes before using them in your cake.

Sprinkle a little flour in the bowl of your scales before measuring treacle, molasses or honey. It will prevent sticking, thus making the scales far easier to clean. Alternatively, rub a little vegetable oil over the bowl for the same result.

There is no need to keep self-raising flour in your cupboard. Simply add two and a half teaspoons of baking soda to every 250g of plain flour and you will get the same effect.

Try adding a teaspoon of white distilled vinegar to your chocolate cake mix.

There is nothing more traditional and satisfying than a home-made apple pie but sometimes the base can become soggy with the moisture released from the fruit. To prevent disappointment, toss the apple chunks in a little plain flour before filling the pie. This works with other fruits as well, not just apples.

If you are out of eggs and you want to make a cake then you can get away with it by adding a tablespoon of white distilled vinegar instead. This method is best used in a recipe which also uses self-raising flour or another kind of raising agent.

Your sponge cake looks delicious but you still have to get it out of the cake tin without it sticking. Stand the tin on a damp cloth for a couple of minutes before attempting to turn it out. This should help.

Heat your spoon with a little boiling water before plunging it into the syrup jar. The syrup will roll off more quickly.

After you've finished baking, rinse your rolling pin, basins, plates and any other objects which have become coated with dry flour in cold water. If you use hot water the flour becomes more sticky and difficult to remove.

All pies need to be pricked to prevent their lids cracking or their juices running over when cooking in the oven. However, small pricks may not do the job required. One ingenious method to get over this is to cut a few slits in the lid of the uncooked pie and stand short lengths of macaroni in them. These will act as vents allowing steam from the hot filling to escape during cooking. Unless you want some interesting comments about the pie, remember to remove the macaroni chimneys before serving.

To improve a pie, all you need to do is add a tablespoon of white distilled vinegar to the pastry recipe.

Adding a drop or two of white distilled vinegar to your sugar icing mix will get you better results.

Add a teaspoon of white distilled vinegar to three egg whites to achieve a fluffier meringue.

Other

To get more juice from your lemons try placing them in boiling water for ten minutes before halving. If you have a microwave then you can pop them in that for a minute to get the same effect. Another method is to squeeze them in your hands before peeling.

When squeezing a lemon directly into your bowl or pan, place a sieve over the top. It will prevent any seeds from getting into the recipe.

To bring out the aromas and flavour of ground spices in a recipe, heat them in a dry pan for a minute or so before using.

Add fresh herbs like parsley and basil at the end of the cooking process just before you serve the meal when the flavours and aromas are at their most pungent. Dried herbs should be added earlier as should 'twiggier' fresh herbs such as rosemary.

Save up the rinds of Parmesan cheese and add them to soups and casseroles during cooking. The rinds will soften and infuse your soups with a deep, but not overpowering, cheesy richness.

Another top tip for soups is to throw in a piece of peel from a citrus fruit. Lemon, lime or orange is good. The result will be subtle but will nonetheless give a lively, zesty lift to the flavour. Remember to pick the peel out of the soup before serving.

Smoked chilli or paprika powder adds a lovely and warming, smoky flavour to soups and stews. Here's a recipe for pumpkin soup, ideal for a hallowe'en:

- Finely chop two onions into a large pan and soften in four tablespoons of olive oil without browning.
- Add the roughly-cut chunks of one pumpkin which has been peeled and deseeded.
- Continue cooking for ten minutes or until the chunks have become soft and squishy.
- Add half to one teaspoon of smoked paprika or chilli powder, depending on taste. You can always add a little more later.
- Pour in a small carton of double cream.
- Give the soup a blast with a hand blender and then push the soup through a sieve and into another pan for a lovely, velvety texture.
- Toast a few of the leftover pumpkin seeds until golden in some olive oil. Sprinkle them on top of the soup as a garnish and then serve.
- Enjoy.

If you have a lot of sandwiches to make and you want to save time as well as butter, then pour half a pint of boiling milk over a pound of butter in a basin. Beat the two together and you will find it spreads much easier.

To keep sandwiches fresh, wrap them in greaseproof paper and cover with a damp, cold cloth.

If you've ever been to a chip shop in Edinburgh you'll be familiar with the question: 'Salt and sauce?' The sauce in question is made by diluting brown sauce with vinegar. You can recreate the Scottish chip shop experience and make your sauce go further by topping up the bottle with vinegar when you've used half of the sauce.

For a light and crispy Japanese-style tempura batter use ice-cold carbonated water and minimal beating. Keeping the water very cold prevents it from soaking up too much oil and the bubbles in the water will help keep the batter light and airy.

If you have mistakenly added too much salt to a soup or a casserole there is no need to despair. Slice an apple as thin as you can and add it to the pot. You will find that the salt is attracted into the apple which can be removed after a little while. If you have no apple then you can try using a potato instead.

If you are making gravy using granules you can wake up the flavour and make it taste more fresh by adding a teaspoon of wine or cider vinegar.

Add a little lemon juice to single cream in order to sour it.

If your ketchup is refusing to flow from the bottle then you need to apply a little engineering. Push a straw to the bottom of the bottle making sure it is long enough to reach out of the bottle's neck. Now when you tip the bottle, air will get right to the bottom and allow the sauce to pour out.

If you find an old batch of stale nuts in the back of your cupboard you can revive them by placing them on a baking tray in a hot oven for ten or fifteen minutes.

Store coffee in your fridge to keep it fresh and make it last longer. Make sure it is kept in an airtight container. This applies to both fresh and instant coffee. For the best flavour however, let the coffee come up to room temperature before using.

If a recipe requires cream and you've run out, don't worry. For a

THE TRADITIONAL HOUSEHOLD HANDBOOK

decent stand-in, just heat four parts milk to one part melted butter.

To prevent a skin forming on custard, sprinkle some sugar over the top after removing the pan from the heat.

Place a sugar cube in your biscuit tin. It will help remove any moistness from the air and keep your biscuits crisp for longer.

Increase the shelf life of your milk by adding a pinch of salt to it after opening. It should last twice as long as usual. Adding a little salt also means you can store it in the freezer.

You can make your bread last a couple of weeks by wrapping it in foil and storing it on the lowest shelf of your fridge.

To prevent your salt from sticking together add a few grains of dried rice to it. The rice will absorb any moisture and keep your salt flowing smoothly.

When boiling a pan of water then remember to keep a lid on it. There will be less loss of heat and the water will boil faster. It's also safer.

Adding salt to a pan of water will make it boil that much faster.

Add some lemon juice to the water when you are boiling rice and it will turn out fluffier and whiter.

You will find it easier to cut a thin slice from your loaf if you dip the bread knife into hot water and then dry before slicing.

If crystals form in your honey you can make them disappear in minutes by placing the pot in a bowl of boiled water. The honey will flow again.

To prevent your pasta from sticking together add a little white distilled vinegar to the boiling water.

You will get fluffier rice if you add a teaspoon of white distilled vinegar to the cooking water.

Remember to give rice a good rinse before boiling. This will help get rid of excess starch.

You can reuse oil from your fryer if you strain it through a coffee filter.

Butter gives a lovely taste to fried foods but is easy to burn in the pan. When frying with butter, be sure to add a little cooking oil as well and it will prevent the butter from burning.

A stale loaf of bread can be used to make bread crumbs. Simply grate the bread and store the crumbs in a plastic bag in your freezer.

Now you will never be without breadcrumbs which can be used in recipes that require crunchy coatings and toppings.

When you've run out of fresh bread and you absolutely need that sandwich you can revive a stale loaf by running cold water over it. All you need to do then is place it in a hot oven for ten minutes.

Mustard powder is cheaper to buy than a pot of ready-mixed English mustard. Add cold water drop by drop and mix until you achieve the desired consistency. Let it stand for ten minutes before using, as this will enhance the heat.

Fresh herbs bought from the shops are expensive but they can go off quickly. To preserve parsley you should wash it in cold water and pat it dry with a clean cloth or some paper towels. Keep it in the fridge in an open-ended plastic bag. Lettuce lasts much longer if you treat it in the same way.

Dried herbs are a must-have in the kitchen for when you cannot get your hands on fresh. Because they are chopped so finely and do not contain any moisture you need to use less than you would fresh, so go easy on them. If they are stored in the light or are exposed to air they will lose colour and flavour, so always keep them in a dark cupboard in an air-tight container. Alternatively, store them in air-tight jars that do not let the light in.

You can put a dollop of mustard in your wok when making a stir-fry to add zinginess.

Don't waste energy when cooking on a hob. Choose the right-sized heating element or gas jet for the size of pan you're using. If the flame is licking around the sides of the pan you are likely to burn food, damage your cooking ware and you will certainly waste heat.

We all know that beans mean flatulence. If you want a less windy aftermath then try adding a couple of teaspoons of cider vinegar to the pan when soaking beans or split peas. Add another couple to the cooking water. Adding half a teaspoon of cider vinegar to a tin of baked beans will also help.

Eggs

You should always remove eggs from the fridge for at least an hour before using.

A fresh egg will lie on its side when placed in the bottom of a bowl of water. If it's more than three days old it stands at an angle and if it has been around for more than ten days it will stand on end.

Fresh eggs hold together much better when poaching. If they are good and fresh you can simply add them to a large pan of gently simmering water. If your eggs are older however, you can still retain their shape by adding a little vinegar or lemon juice to the water. Make a whirlpool in the water by swirling a spoon around in the pan and then drop the egg into the middle. The white will twist around the yolk forming a pleasing end product.

Too much beating will make your omelette rubbery. Stop before the white and yolk are completely combined. Being able to see yellow and white streaks in the finished omelette makes it more attractive.

It's easy to peel a hard-boiled egg if you stand it in iced water for a minute after cooking and then pop it back into the pan of boiled water for a few seconds. The cold causes the egg to shrink from its shell and then the hot water makes the shell expand.

An egg white will thicken faster if you add a pinch of salt before beating.

To slice hard-boiled eggs, dip your knife in hot water first. It will prevent the yolk from crumbling.

Sometimes, recipes require the white of an egg only. You can keep the yolks fresh for a couple of days by slipping them carefully into a bowl of fresh water and storing them in a cool place. Your fridge would be ideal.

Hard-boiled eggs can become discoloured when exposed to air. To keep them white, place them in a bowl of cold water as soon as the shell is removed.

Eggs can crack when being boiled. To stop this happening, simply add a few drops of vinegar to the water.

Instead of milk, add a tablespoon of water to your eggs before beating. Your omelettes will turn out more light and fluffy.

COOKING WITH ESSENTIAL OILS

I first discovered essential oils a couple of years ago and have found many uses for them in the kitchen.

You can buy this fragrant treasure in health food stores. It is usually extracted from plants via steam distillation but with some fruits they can be obtained by pressing. For example, if you twist a piece of lemon rind you will see a little oily liquid come out which smells strongly of lemon. That is the fruit's essential oil.

There are many claims as to the health benefits of essential oils. Here I will concentrate only on their ability to add fragrance and taste, thus making an everyday meal into something altogether more special.

Mayonnaise

You can add essential oils to basic mayonnaise to achieve a host of wonderful effects. Here's a recipe for basic mayonnaise:

You will need one egg yolk, half a teaspoon of Dijon mustard, a quarter teaspoon of salt, a quarter teaspoon of black pepper, one teaspoon of white wine vinegar and 100ml of olive oil. You will also need a mixing bowl and a hand whisk or fork.

- Mix all the ingredients in a bowl except for the olive oil.
- Slowly and continuously add the oil while whisking gently in one direction.
- Continue to add the oil until the mayonnaise reaches the desired consistency.

Now you know how to make mayonnaise you can add some fun to the process by using essential oils.

Try chopping some garlic and adding four drops of lime essential oil to the bowl for a zingy dip.

Add a couple of drops of fennel essential oil for a wonderful accompaniment to fish.

Some sage essential oil in mayonnaise will go very well with cold chicken.

Orangey Chocolate

Melt some chocolate in a bowl and add a few drops of orange essential oil to make orange-flavoured chocolate. You can substitute the orange oil for peppermint. Just let your imagination and your taste buds go wild. One tip for melting chocolate is to put it in a bowl and then place the bowl in a pan of hot water.

Essential Oils and Butter

By combining a drop or three of your desired essential oil with some butter you can bring vegetables to life. Try ginger butter on green beans for a taste sensation. Again, you are only limited by your imagination.

Bread

If you're into making your own bread then you can make it extra special by adding a few drops of rosemary essential oil.

SECTION 5

Gardening

A garden can provide many hours of pleasure. There is something deeply pleasurable about the process of planting, nurturing and harvesting. Everyone, from small child to octogenerian, can appreciate this.

Perhaps it is about being in tune with your environment. There is nothing like a garden for making you aware of the changing of the seasons and the cycle of life. I think it helps us to understand our place in the world.

Gardening is a past-time in which you are always learning and it helps to keep your mind and body lively. There is no substitute for experience but that does not mean you cannot learn from the experience of others. What follows is a collection of wisdom that began to accumulate for me, by spending weekends with grandad on his allotment.

KNOW YOUR SOIL

The key to a healthy garden is healthy soil. Think of it as the blank canvas upon which you can paint your design. First you need to prepare it. There are two things to consider – the texture of the soil and whether it is acidic or alkaline.

Some plants prefer acidic soil and some less so. Having a look at the weeds in your garden will give some indication as to its level. Creeping buttercup, sorrel, dock, nettle and mare's tail all thrive in acidic soils. However, it is worth buying a soil testing kit. They are inexpensive and available from garden centres.

Most plants prefer slightly acidic soil – between 6.5 and 7.0 on the pH scale. Potatoes thrive better when it is slightly more acidic, whereas cabbages and others in the brassica family prefer it slightly more alkaline. Note that a pH of 7.0 is neutral.

If you want to use plants for which the soil type is not ideal, you can change the conditions. It's usually easier to make soil more alkaline than it is to make it more acidic, although it's best to make it a long-term project. Test your soil each year and make adjustments gradually. You can add lime, hardwood ash, bonemeal or crushed oyster shells to raise the soil pH and make it more alkaline.

To lower the soil pH (or make it more acidic), use sawdust, composted leaves, wood chips or leaf mould.

Do not mix fertiliser with an alkaline as they will react. A good time to lime is in the autumn. You can add fertiliser the following spring.

The second consideration when it comes to soil type is whether it is sandy, clay or – the ideal type – loam. Unlike sandy soil, loam will retain moisture but not become waterlogged like clay.

You can add humus – that is composted vegetation – to improve the soil and make it more loamy.

COMPOST CORNER

Experienced gardeners get passionate about compost. Adding it to your soil improves it no end. Not for them the expensive variety you find in your local gardening centre. Certainly not for us either, not when you can make your own from kitchen and garden waste.

There's no need to worry about bad smells or rats if you follow a few simple tips. Composting occurs naturally. It is the reason the world is not piled high with dead trees and plants. Essentially, it is worms that turn rotting vegetable matter into soil. There is nothing smelly or dirty about it. Just remember not to add meat or any cooked food to the pile. It is this that will attract rats or foxes.

You will need to find a place to compost in. There are a few options. You can buy one of those Dalek-style bins which are fine for a small garden. Alternatively, you can make one by upturning a rubbish bin and cutting a hole in the top. Use a wooden board as a lid and weight it down with a brick. Another option is to make one using three pallets. Just remember that all compost bins need to be situated on soil so that the worms can get in and do their job.

If you have a big garden then the pallet option is perhaps the best. Just stand them on their edge so that you have a box shape with the front side missing. Use some wire or rope to bind them together. You might want to get hold of some plastic sheeting to cover the heap as it builds. This will help to retain heat which will help with the rotting down process. It will also prevent the resulting compost from becoming too soggy in the rain.

Whenever you mow the lawn you add the cuttings to the pile. If you're not too squeamish you can add wee to the pile which will give the composting a helping hand. When you've finished raking fallen leaves, add them to the pile too.

A good rule of thumb is to try not to put too much of one thing in the pile as a glut may destroy its balance. Variety is the spice of good compost.

Give your compost a good turning over every now and again. The microbes which help it rot down will appreciate the oxygen this adds to the pile.

Keep a Tupperware box with a sealable lid in your kitchen. Whenever you peel vegetables put the peelings in the box. Tea bags can go in there if you rip them apart first. Add scrunched up egg shells to it. Tear up the finished egg carton while you're at it. This can go in as well. Adding cardboard or straw will ensure the heap does not get too wet, but try not to add card or paper with print on it. What you're after is a nice crumbly texture to your compost. When your kitchen box is full, add the contents to the compost heap or bin.

You can use your lovely compost to spread all over your soil. It will add humus and structure as well as providing nutrients to your growing plants.

MULCH

A mulch is something spread over the surface of your soil to keep moisture from evaporating out of it in dry weather and to suppress weeds. It really does cut down on the amount of watering you have to do and is particularly useful if you are going to be away from your garden for a few days in hot weather.

Ideally, a good mulch should also leach nutrients into the earth to give your plants extra food when growing and it should help to improve the structure of your soil. A favourite mulch of gardeners is leaf mould but you need to be thinking ahead in order to collect it.

Leaf mould forms when fallen leaves go mouldy. In the autumn, collect leaves in black plastic bags. Tie the bags off and leave them until the spring. Spread your leaf mould around the base of bushes and established plants. Put it all over your beds and it will suppress weed growth.

You can use wood chippings or even cardboard sheets as mulch but good old leaf mould is the best.

NATURAL FERTILISERS

You can make some wonderful fertilisers from 'weeds' that grow in your garden, including nettles, comfrey and dandelions.

NETTLE TEA

Nettles are full of calcium, copper, iron, phosphorous and nitrogen, all the things your plants really appreciate. You need to stuff a bucket, barrel or even an old plastic drinks bottle with nettles and then cover them with water. Rainwater is better than tap water as it contains no added chemicals but don't worry too much about it. Tap water will be fine.

Cover your bucket or barrel and leave well alone for four or five weeks. The resulting tea will stink to high heaven. Strain the liquid once it has brewed. You can pour it neat onto your compost heap. If you are using it to fertilise growing plants it will be far too strong so will need diluting, add one part nettle tea to ten parts fresh water.

COMFREY TEA

Once upon a time every amateur garden would include a patch of comfrey growing in a disused corner to be used as a fertiliser or even as a medicinal herb. (Its old-fashioned country name is Knitbone as it was used to treat people with broken bones.)

It's a very hardy plant that will grow in anything from full sun to almost full shade. You need to be careful where you grow it however, as its roots travel way underground and a new plant will grow from even a small piece of broken-off root.

It is its deep roots – able to search out nutrients other plants cannot reach – that make comfrey such a good fertiliser. The leaves are full of nitrogen, phosphorous and potassium.

To make tea from the leaves you need to use the same method as with nettles. A word of warning though: If anything, comfrey tea smells even worse than the nettle variety, so make sure you brew it somewhere out of the way of delicate nostrils. Remember to dilute it with ten parts water to one part tea when using it to feed plants.

Tomatoes absolutely love it. Start feeding them once the first fruits appear. Once a week should be enough for them. It will make for healthier and tastier crops.

You can also use fresh comfrey leaves to line the trench in which you will grow potatoes.

You can split a comfrey plant by driving a spade through the middle of it. Cut its roots into three inch lengths and plant them. Another comfrey plant will result from each piece of root.

DANDELION TEA

You can make a good fertilising tea from dandelions as well. Like comfrey they have deep, searching roots that will delve for nutrients. When using dandelions to make tea, ensure you do not use the seed heads. That is because if you do not 'brew' them for long enough the seeds may survive and you will spread them all over your vegetable patch and flower beds.

COMPANION PLANTING

Have you ever noticed how you seem to thrive more around some people rather than others? Quite often you will work better with someone who has completely different qualities to yourself. It's because you make a good team. Should you have any shortcomings in one area, your team-mate can cover you and vice versa.

There is a similar dynamic with plants. Growing certain varieties together brings mutual benefits in terms of health and vigour and a reduction in problems with pests and disease. It's something that gardeners have known about for generations and they use their knowledge to get better crops and displays. Applying this accumulated wisdom is known as companion or complementary planting.

There are several ways in which plants can complement each other:

- Some will give off a chemical from their roots or foliage that repels pests that would otherwise attack their companion.
- Others will attract good insects that will help to pollinate a companion plant or keep it pest-free.
- Some will add nutrients to the soil for the benefit of their companion.
- Yet more will grow tall providing shelter or support for those next to them, or cover the ground suppressing weeds and retaining moisture for a drought-prone companion.
- Others may act as a honey trap for pests, diverting them away from the plant you want to protect.

A classic example of companion planting is the 'Three Sisters' method of growing squash, sweetcorn and French beans together. In this case the sweetcorn grows tall and provides support for the French beans to climb. Little nodules that form on the roots of the bean plant are packed with nitrogen that will feed the soil for the benefit of others in years to come. The squash meanwhile, will creep around and cover the ground forming a living mulch. This will help to retain moisture in the soil for its 'sisters' to drink and suppress weeds. Each one has a role to play.

THREE SISTERS METHOD

Before we look at some more combinations, here's how you can try the 'Three Sisters' method in your own vegetable patch.

Choose a site that basks in full sun for at least six hours a day. To ensure your corn forms full and juicy cobs there need to be enough plants. For that reason you will ideally have a ten by ten foot patch. It will still work with fewer sweetcorn plants but the cobs are unlikely to be fully pollinated.

- Add plenty of compost or aged manure to the patch as the nitrogen from the beans will not be released until the following year.
- Mark off three ten foot rows, five feet apart.
- Build mounds of earth that are 18 inches across and flattened on top. Stagger them across the rows so that there are three in the first row, two in the second and three in the third.
- Upon each mound, plant four sweetcorn seeds at the corners of an imaginary six inch square.
- When the corn reaches about four inches tall, weed the patch. Now is the time to plant the beans and the squash.
- Plant four bean seeds in each mound with each seed about three or four inches away from its sweetcorn neighbour.
- Between each mound, build another one to plant your squash seeds in. These should be planted at the corners of an imaginary triangle about four inches apart.
- Once the squash seedlings emerge, remove the weakest looking one.
- You will need to weed regularly until the squash covers the ground and does the job for you.

MORE PLANTS TO GROW TOGETHER

- If you plant garlic among roses its smell will help to ward off aphids.
- The roots of African marigolds produce a chemical that will reduce attacks on tomatoes from nematodes, slugs and wireworms. Their smell will also put off attacks from greenfly and blackfly.
- Chinese cabbage, once it has gone to seed, will attract aphids away from your other cabbage varieties.
- Grow sage with carrots or cabbage, sprouts and broccoli. The strong scents of these plants will put each others pests off.
- Nasturtiums are attractive to caterpillars and they will be

diverted away from your cabbages.
- Leeks repel carrot fly and carrots are horrible to onion fly and leek moth. Grow them together.
- Chervil will keep aphids from attacking your lettuce.
- Asparagus will deter nematodes from attacking tomato plant roots.
- The strong smell of chives will protect your chrysanthemums, sunflowers and tomatoes from aphid attack.
- Members of the pea and bean family, including the ornamental sweet pea, take nitrogen from the air and store it in nodules on their roots. Leave their roots in the ground when the plant has died off and dig them in. The added nitrogen will boost the growth of anything that is planted afterwards.
- Dill will attract hoverflies and predatory wasps which will eat aphids that dare to enter your plot.
- Plants with brightly-coloured flowers will attract bees to pollinate your vegetables.
- Yarrow will attract ladybirds and their larvae to your garden. Ladybirds love to eat aphids.
- Tansy will deter ants from nesting.
- Basil repels flies and mosquitos and makes an ideal companion for tomato plants.
- Rosemary puts off cabbage white butterflies, bean beetle and carrot fly.

INCOMPATIBLE PLANTS

Some people you just don't get on with. They bring out the worst in you. Again, there is a similar dynamic in the plant world.

Did you know that potatoes and tomatoes belong to the same family? Experienced gardeners never plant them close together as they are susceptible to the same diseases – like blight – that can spread easily between the two. Here are a few more that should never be bedfellows:

- Onions, beets, kohlrabi and sunflower should not be grown near runner or broad beans.

- Dill, strawberries, runner beans and tomatoes should not be grown near members of the cabbage family which includes sprouts and broccoli.
- Do not grow cucumbers near potatoes or aromatic herbs.
- Members of the onion family, gladioli and potatoes should not be planted near peas.
- Do not plant dill near celery.

LAWNS

A lush and well-kept lawn will set off your flower beds but a badly mown lawn will be an eyesore. Regular mowing will encourage thicker and lusher lawn growth but there are a few things you need to bear in mind.

Do not mow during the hottest part of the day as the cut ends of the grass will tend to scorch in hot sunlight. Instead, you should mow in the morning or the late afternoon.

It is never a good idea to get your mower out if the grass is wet. First off, there is the obvious danger of electrocution. But it is not just you who might end up looking a little frazzled. Wet grass tends to clump around the blades of the mower, clogging it up and causing you to tear the grass out of the ground rather than cutting it.

For the same reason you should try to keep the blades of your mower nice and sharp. It is good practice to sharpen them at the end of the gardening season so that they are ready to go when it comes to the first cut of the spring.

You will need to remove them from your lawnmower. Keep them held tightly in a vice and use a file to get the required edge.

Mowers are not really designed for cutting grass that has grown to much more than three inches in height, so a regular cut is essential for a smart-looking lawn. However, there will be several weeks between the last cut of the summer and the first of spring when the grass may exceed this height. When attempting the first cut of the year it is probably best to set your mower at the highest level. Then, give it another going-over with the blades set lower down.

MORE TOP TIPS FOR YOUR GARDEN

If you are short on space or growing in a backyard you can still grow vegetables in pots. There is a great tip for growing potatoes in a backyard using old car tyres:

- Lay a flattened cardboard box on the ground and place an old car tyre on top.
- Fill the tyre with compost, making sure it fills the rim completely, and plant a seed potato in it.
- Once the plant has grown to about six inches, place another tyre on top of the first and fill again with compost so that only the tip of the potato plant is showing.
- Repeat the process until you have filled three or four tyres.
- Harvesting is easy. Simply kick the tyres over and pick the spuds from the roots.

SAFE AND COLOURFUL CANES

There is many a tale of gardeners bending down and damaging their faces and eyes on the ends of canes placed in the ground to support growing plants. A wonderfully colourful solution is to get hold of a bag of children's ball-pit balls. These hollow plastic balls are sold by the bagful in toy shops but you are likely to find them sold in pound stores if you keep your eyes peeled. Simply poke a hole in a ball and place it over the end of the cane. The result is a pretty, colourful and safe vegetable patch.

MEASURE BY MEASURE

Vegetables and flowers need space to reach their potential. Seed packets will normally give you a guide as to how far apart they should be planted. Rather than carrying a tape measure around with you, a more convenient way to measure distances is to mark them on a long-handled tool such as a rake. Simply notch the handle with a knife or mark with permanent ink.

WEED OR VEGETABLE SEEDLING?

It can be very difficult telling whether those green shoots sprouting in your vegetable patch are weeds or the beginning of a future meal, particularly if you are growing the variety of vegetable for the first time.

To prevent pulling up your prized seedlings it is a good idea to be organised when sowing them in the first place. Peg out a length of string and sow along it. You can use a lolly stick to mark the row. Write the planting date and the type of veg you are growing. When the seedlings start to appear they will come up in a straight line and you will know they are not weeds.

FREE BRAZIER

Some garden waste cannot be composted and the best way to get rid of it is by burning. When burning waste, a brazier makes it easier to contain the fire. It is also safer and less damaging to your garden than digging a fire pit. If you can get hold of an old washing machine drum it will make an excellent brazier. The small holes around the drum, which in its previous life allowed the washing water to escape, give a fantastic air supply to the fire.

WOOD ASH

Once you've finished burning waste wood, do not throw the ashes away. Wood ash is full of nutrients and can be spread over your soil or even better, added to your compost heap. Do not use the ash from treated or painted wood in your compost heap as it could contain nasty chemicals.

PATHS

If you sprinkle salt between the cracks of paving stones in paths it will act as a weedkiller.

You can make a good temporary path to get you between the sections of your vegetable plot with wood chippings. These will eventually rot down and if you dig them in will help provide structure to your soil.

Alternatively, you can use stones. It is a good idea to remove stones from your beds, particularly if you plan to grow root vegetables such as carrots and parsnips which will split if they encounter one. Remove as many stones as you can with a garden sieve. Keep them together in an old compost bag and when you have enough, make a path out of them.

If you have some old bricks to hand you can use these to make a temporary path through your vegetable plot.

PLASTIC GARDEN FURNITURE

You need somewhere to sit and enjoy your garden. The great advantage of plastic furniture is it can be left outdoors in all weather without warping. It can, however, become discoloured and will need a good clean every now and again. The best thing to do is to squeeze a couple of tablespoons of ordinary washing-up liquid into four table-spoons of bleach. Give all the surfaces a good wipe down using a cloth. Wear rubber gloves to protect your hands from the bleach. Leave the solution on the furniture for half an hour or so and then rinse with fresh water.

FENCE POSTS

Wooden fence posts are susceptible to rotting in the ground. To make them last longer, make sure you treat the base to a good coating of linseed oil mixed with powdered charcoal before planting.

FISH-FANCIER'S FAVOURITE

If you keep fish in an aquarium then you have an excellent source of plant food on tap. Whenever you change the water don't throw the old lot down the sink. Instead, use it to water flower beds. The nutrients in the water will help make your flowers blooming lovely. Alternatively, you can pour this rich liquid over your compost heap.

WATERING

Water your plants first thing in the morning or last thing in the evening. Doing this will prevent wasting water through evaporation. Not only that, if water splashes onto the leaves in strong sunlight they can become scorched. This is a particular problem with delicate leaves.

REUSE YOUR POTS

Plastic plant pots can be reused but to ensure any diseases present are not passed onto the next occupant they need to be sterilised first. Give them a good soaking in a bucket of water to which a cupful of white distilled vinegar has been added. Let them soak for an hour.

GARDEN HOSES

When storing your garden hose over the winter, first make sure there is no water left in it. If there is it could freeze and if this happens it is likely to expand and cause the hose to split. Keep it in your shed as the temperature in there is likely to be a couple of degrees higher than outside during the cold nights.

TOOLS

It is better to buy garden tools in the winter when they are likely to be on sale or cheaper than they are in the spring.

It is important to look after your tools. A clean spade for example, will dig with far less effort than one left caked in mud or rust. To remove rust from your tools use a soap-filled steel-wool pad dipped in paraffin. Finish off by rubbing with a crumpled-up piece of aluminium foil.

SPACE SAVER

You can double the shelf space in your shed by using the underside of them as well as storing things on top. You will need to collect jam jars and screw their lids to the underside of your shelf. Once you've done this you can screw the jars onto their lids. This is an excellent way of storing seed packets, screws, nails, bits of garden twine and any other bits and bobs.

FLY AWAY

You can prevent your shed or greenhouse from becoming a retirement home for insects by spraying corners and surfaces with full-strength white distilled vinegar.

CUT FLOWERS AND INDOOR PLANTS

Cut Flowers

Add a few drops of bleach to the water of cut flowers. It will keep the water clear, prevent stagnation, keep your vase clean and will have no adverse affect on the flowers. A small piece of charcoal in the water will also prevent it from clouding up.

If the stems on your cut flowers are too short to display properly in your vase, slip their ends into a drinking straw and cut it to the desired height.

Add a copper coin to the water in the vase when displaying daffodils and they will last longer. Never display daffodils in water with other flowers as they contain a toxin that will kill off vase-mates.

When cutting flowers, make a diagonal cut with sharp scissors or a knife. This gives a greater surface area for the water to get into the stem than a straight cut. Trim the stems under water to prevent bubbles forming and impeding the take-up of water.

You can extend the life of cut tulips by making a series of small holes down their stems.

Strip away the lower leaves of chrysanthemums and split the end of the stem before putting in a vase of water. They will last longer.

Indoor Plants

You can use the water from boiling eggs to water your house

plants. If you leave the crushed-up egg shells in it for a few days before watering the plants it will be even better.

Flowers and plants turn their heads and leaves towards the sun. To keep your house plants growing straight and true you should rotate the pots by a quarter turn every day so they absorb the sun evenly.

For glossy- and healthy-looking leaves on plants such as mother-in-law's tongue, wipe the foliage every month or so with a damp cloth dipped in almond oil. This is a particularly good regime to follow if your house is centrally heated.

Bury a couple of cloves of garlic in your plant pots to deter greenfly.

When watering your house plants be careful not to get any on the leaves. This is particularly important if they are going to be in strong sunlight as their leaves will get scorched.

If you are going away for a while you will need to make sure your house plants remain well-watered. Never mind if you do not have a neighbour to do the job. Instead, place a container filled with water near the plants and trail a length of thick wool between it and the pot to be watered. The wool will absorb the water along its length and slowly but surely, drip into the pot.

Alternatively, soak an old towel with water and place it in your bath. Stand all your pots on the towel. To ensure the water does not evaporate away too quickly simply cover the towel in plastic sheeting or bags wherever there is space between the pots.

An A-Z of Health

There are plenty of over-the-counter pills, potions and lotions on the market, but back in the old days they managed to do without. My grandmother passed many traditional health tips on to me and I've added many more over the years and collected them here. What I would like to stress, however, is that you should always get the advice of your doctor before following them.

What follows is an A-Z of conditions and some old-fashioned techniques for treating them.

ACNE

Garlic is an antiseptic. An old-fashioned trick to combat acne is to halve a clove and hold the cut end against the spot for several minutes. Make sure you wash the affected area before applying the garlic.

To treat spots you can add a little hydrogen peroxide to some baking powder to make a very thick paste. Dab it on before you go to bed and rinse off in the morning.

ALCOHOL CRAVINGS

You can reduce the desire for alcohol by using a couple of plants which should be available in your nearest health food shop. Make a tea by pouring boiling water over Golden Seal (*Hydrastis Canadensis*) and Goldthread (also known as Canker Root).

APPETITE

Bay leaves are said to stimulate appetite.

To suppress appetite, try taking a tablespoon of safflower oil mixed with two tablespoons of grapefruit juice before meals. Another useful appetite suppressant is to drink a glass of water with a teaspoon of apple cider vinegar in it. You might want to add a little honey to sweeten.

ARTERIES

Atherosclerosis, also known as arteriosclerotic vascular disease (ASVD) is the thickening of the artery walls as a result of the build-up of fatty materials such as cholesterol. Omega 3 oils, found in oily fish such as mackerel and sardine help protect against the build-up of these dangerous fats, so make sure you include them in your diet.

Some people swear by the benefits of apple cider vinegar as a preventative measure. Although no studies have taken place to prove its effectiveness, there can be no harm in drinking a glass of water with one tablespoon of vinegar added every day.

ARTHRITIS

Arthritis can be extremely painful and debilitating and any relief has to be a good thing. A good, hot bath can really take the edge off the pain. Try adding a couple of cups of apple cider vinegar to your bath water, being careful not to get any in your eyes.

My grandmother suffered with pain in her hands. Her solution, which she swore by, was to make up a warm drink of honey, whisky and apple cider vinegar before she went to bed. She also slept like a log.

Cayenne pepper increases the blood flow to the areas upon which it is applied externally and can be used to treat the pain of swollen joints and arthritis. Make a linament to treat the symptoms of arthritis by boiling a pint of apple cider vinegar and adding a tablespoon of cayenne pepper.

ASPIRIN

Aspirin has been shown to reduce the risk of a second stroke or heart attack in those who have already had one. It can, however, cause acid indigestion. If this is the case with you, then you should consider adding a small amount of baking soda to the glass of water you use to take the pill. Baking soda is a good antacid. In other words, it counteracts stomach acidity.

ATHLETE'S FOOT

We've seen how baking soda is a great remedy for cleaning and getting rid of mould in the kitchen. Athlete's foot is a fungal condition and can also be treated with this powder. Try sprinkling some in your socks and shoes.

You can also apply it directly to the affected parts. You will need to make up a paste with water and smooth it where needed. Leave it for ten to twenty minutes before rinsing with clean water. It is a good idea to carry out this process a couple of times a day until the problem disappears.

BLEEDING CUTS AND GRAZES

You can stop the blood flowing from minor cuts and grazes by sprinkling a little cayenne pepper to the wound.

Clean minor cuts with a paste of baking soda and water. Rub it in well before rinsing. Reapply if necessary.

BLOOD

Here's an old recipe for nettle syrup – said to be a blood purifier – that was found written in faded ink in an album in a Cumbrian farmhouse. Gather the tops of young nettles and wash well. For every 1 lb of nettles add a quart of water. Boil in a pot for an hour and strain. For every pint of juice add 1 lb of sugar. Boil for a further 30 minutes, leave it to cool and then bottle it.

BLOOD CIRCULATION

Cayenne pepper thins the blood. If you have problems with circulation then make sure you add plenty to your food. This is particularly useful if you enjoy hot and spicy food. If not, try using paprika instead, as it is milder.

BLOOD PRESSURE

If you have high blood pressure, drink cayenne tea up to three times a day. Another way to lower the pressure is to drink two teaspoons of apple cider vinegar in water. Sweeten it with honey to improve the taste.

BURNS

Minor burns can be treated with water. Place the burned area in a bowl of cold water, preferably ice cold and leave until there is no heat left in the burn. If this is impossible then you need to soak a clean towel in the water and hold it to the affected part. Keep on refreshing the towel as it is the cold that is the key to this treatment.

If you have some baking soda handy then you should add some to the water and it will help prevent the skin from blistering.

CHILBLAINS

Rub chilblains twice daily with a cut onion dipped in salt.

COLDS, FLU, COUGHS AND SORE THROATS

To keep colds and flu at bay drink a cup of cayenne pepper tea three times a day at the first sign of a problem. Simply add half a teaspoon to a mug of hot water.

Dissolve cayenne pepper powder in water or boil whole cayenne peppers in water to improvise a gargling solution for sore throats.

Chewing on a piece of raw onion can destroy germs in the mouth within five minutes and can be good for colds and sore throats.

Instead of paying out for expensive cough medicines there is a better way to get rid of the phlegm associated with colds and flu. Mix up a tablespoon of honey, a dessertspoon of apple cider vinegar, and the oil from a garlic capsule. Take a teaspoon of the mixture before meals and before retiring to bed for the night.

A dry, ticklish and persistent cough can be very irritating. Here's a solution for you: Fill a mug half-and-half with apple cider vinegar and water. Stir in a beaten egg. Season the concoction with salt and pepper. Take a good sip every few minutes and you should begin to get some relief. You can reduce the amount of vinegar to a quarter of a cup if you wish.

If you know a beekeeper then ask them for some propolis. This is a resinous substance collected from plants by bees which the insects use to plug gaps and strengthen the structure of the hive. Beekeepers have long recommended keeping a piece in the mouth as a lozenge for sore throats.

CONSTIPATION

Eat plenty of raw apples if you are prone to constipation. You could also try mixing some honey and a teaspoon of apple cider vinegar in some hot water. Drink it with your breakfast.

Parsley is a mild laxative and will help you to digest your food.

Another simple thing to try is to drink a couple of glasses of warm water first thing in the morning.

My favourite old-fashioned constipation cure is this mild laxative jam made from prunes: De-stone 1 lb of prunes and add to 1 lb of raisins and ½ lb of blanched almonds. Add the kernels from the prune stones. Chop everything together as fine as you can or use a blender and leave overnight in a pint of water. Next day add 1 lb of demerara sugar and bring to the boil before simmering gently for 30 minutes. Pour into jars and seal immediately.

CYSTITIS

Add a teaspoon of baking soda to a glass of hot water. Drink one glass every hour for three hours. It will help kill the germs and reduce inflammation.

DANDRUFF

Massage lavender vinegar into your scalp before washing with your usual shampoo and repeat every day until your dandruff disappears. You can also use this method to prevent dandruff in the first place but only do it a couple of times a week.

DIARRHOEA

If you need to go the toilet all the time it is probably because your body is trying to get rid of something that is irritating the digestive system. The last thing you want to do is stop the evacuation altogether. However, if you wish to control the symptoms and lessen their intensity, then try taking a teaspoon of apple cider vinegar in a glass of water.

EARACHE

If earache is caused by a build-up of wax you can treat it by making up a solution of equal parts of white distilled vinegar and almond oil. Heat the solution to body temperature and apply to the ears with a dropper. Don't delve around too much with cotton wool buds as you could damage your eardrum.

FEET

If you're feet are cold you can warm them by sprinkling cayenne pepper into your socks. This will increase the circulation to your feet.

To get rid of foot odour you should try sprinkling baking soda in your socks and shoes.

If your feet are hard and calloused you should begin a bathing regime. Fill a bowl with warm water. Next, add about half a cup of white distilled vinegar and some Epsom salts. Soak your feet for half an hour or so. They should become nice and soft if you do this every evening for a month. You'll also feel a lot more relaxed due to the pampering.

If you've been on your feet all day, any kind of foot bath will feel like a relaxing balm. Add a couple of tablespoons of baking soda for a lovely, cleaning and softening effect.

FEVER

It sounds bizarre, but if you soak a pair of socks in equal parts of apple cider vinegar and cold water, wring them out and then place them on the feet of a person with a fever, it helps bring it down. Resoak the socks before they dry out and put them on again.

FIGHTING FAT

Take a tiny sip of apple cider vinegar with your meal as it helps to prevent you absorbing the fat in food as it passes through your digestive system.

FLATULENCE

You can overcome wind by drinking a cup of caraway seed tea after meals. Add a little apple cider vinegar to the water you use when cooking beans.

GUM DISEASE

Make a paste of two parts baking soda and one part hydrogen peroxide. Use your toothbrush to work it gently over your gums. Do this once or twice a day.

HAIR

To keep your scalp well-served with good blood circulation and stimulate hair growth you should turn to cayenne pepper powder. Try it every day. Simply add one quarter of a teaspoon of the pepper to a teaspoon of baby oil and massage it into the scalp.

If your scalp is dry, then carrying out a simple regime before washing your hair will help. Take four parts of Vaseline or another brand of petroleum jelly and add one part baking soda. Massage it into your scalp and leave for a quarter of an hour before washing it out.

HAY FEVER

Try getting hold of some honey from a local beekeeper. The pollen collected by the bees to make the honey is the same as that which makes you sneeze and you will build up a tolerance by taking a teaspoon of honey a couple of times a day. Start taking your honey before the hay fever season begins.

HEADACHE

Breathe in the steam from a bowl of hot water with apple cider vinegar added. Take between 50 and 100 deep breaths.

HICCUPS

Drinking water from the far side of my cup always cures an attack of hiccups for me. Other cures are said to be sucking on a sugar lump or swallowing a teaspoon of vinegar.

INDIGESTION

Baking soda makes a marvellous antacid. Just add half a teaspoon to a glass of water and drink it down straight away. Leave a couple of hours between doses and do not repeat more than seven times in 24 hours.

INSECT BITES AND STINGS

If it's a bee that has taken a fancy to you, you will need to remove the sting and venom sac as these are left behind in the skin. This should be done as soon as possible. Use the back of your thumbnail to scrape along your skin, getting underneath the barb of the sting, and flick it off. Under no circumstances should you squeeze the venom sac as this will only inject more of the toxin into you.

Make up a paste of baking soda and apple cider vinegar. The baking soda will ease the pain and the vinegar will help destroy the poison in the sting. Apply it to the area affected for relief. This also works well with ant bites and other stinging insects. It does not work on wasp stings, however.

Wasps do not leave their stinger behind so you do not need to worry about getting it out. Instead, apply some lemon juice to the affected area. You can also use diluted vinegar.

INSOMNIA

You can relieve insomnia by eating a boiled onion at bedtime. Another thing you could try is to raise the level of your feet while sleeping. Placing a cushion under the mattress at the foot of your bed will help the blood flow back to your heart.

A cup of camomile tea before bed will help you get off to sleep.

ITCHY SKIN

Soak a clean cloth in a half-and-half apple cider vinegar and water solution and then wring it out. Gently place the cloth on itchy skin for relief, remembering to wash it off with clean water.

JELLYFISH STINGS

If you are stung by a jellyfish at the seaside, wash with seawater and then find the nearest fish and chip shop and ask to borrow some vinegar. Apply to the sting. It is a good idea to get some medical advice as well.

MENSTRUATION

If you suffer from considerable period pain you should consider cutting down on meat and wheat before and during menstruation. To combat irregular periods and excessive bleeding, take a couple of teaspoons of apple cider vinegar diluted in a glass of water two or three times a day.

MUSCLE PAIN

You can use cayenne peppers as a pain-relieving muscle rub. They contain capsaicin which stimulates nerve endings to produce the chemical that transmits pain signals to the brain. You will feel a warm or even hot sensation when this happens. Once the nerve endings have sent out all the chemical warnings there will be none left to send further pain signals.

To take advantage of this effect, mix half a teaspoon of cayenne pepper with a teaspoon of baby oil. Massage the linament into the area affected by muscle pain.

NAUSEA

Take ginger cordial for relief from feelings of nausea.

NERVES

Camomile tea helps relieve nervous tension. Marjoram tea is good for nervous hysteria. Bananas are also said to be good for those of a nervous disposition.

NETTLE AND POISON IVY STINGS

Nettles are covered in hollow hairs that stick to your skin when you come into contact with them. The hairs contain chemical irritants. You can use sticky tape to pull most of them out. Simply place the tape over the area and pull it off again.

Nettle stings are acidic and so can be countered with an alkaline substance. A paste of baking soda and water can be applied to the sting to reduce the pain. You can also try rubbing the juice from the cut end of a cucumber or from parsley onto the affected area. Take it slowly and rub gently.

Look out for the big and broad leaves of the dock plant, which often grows close to nettles. Snap off a leaf with a little stem left on it. Chew or twist the end of the stem to break down the fibres and allow some of its juice to escape. Rub the rash gently with the bruised end of the stem.

You can treat rashes caused by contact with poison ivy in the same way you would treat those caused by nettles.

NEURALGIA

We've seen how cayenne pepper works as a muscle rub when mixed with baby oil and you can take advantage of the same properties to reduce pain associated with neuralgia.

PICK-ME-UP

For a refreshing summer tonic, pour boiling water over some fresh mint leaves. Add a little honey for sweetness.

PILES

You can reduce the pain of haemorrhoids by using plenty of cayenne pepper in your cooking.

RHEUMATISM

Place a muslin bag filled with marjoram in your bath water to relieve the stiffness associated with rheumatism.

SMOKING (HOW TO STOP)

Eating a raw apple or a handful of grapes is said to reduce nicotine cravings. If you buy a bunch of grapes in the morning instead of a pack of cigarettes you could be at the beginning of a smoke-free life.

Add half a teaspoon of Rochelle salts to a half teaspoon of cream of tartar and take it before breakfast. This is said to reduce nicotine cravings for the day.

An emergency 'craving-capper', which should not be used more than twice a day, involves our old favourite, baking soda. When you are feeling the symptoms of nicotine withdrawal you need to dunk two teaspoons of baking soda in a glass of water. Drink the solution down while it's still fizzing away.

SPLINTERS

Place an ice-cube over the splinter and this will numb the skin enough to remove it without pain.

SPRAINS

Heat some soda water with apple cider vinegar and a big pinch of salt. Soak a bandage in the solution and wring it out before using it to wrap the sprain.

STOMACH UPSETS

An upset tummy can be cured by taking a couple of teaspoons of apple cider vinegar in a glass of water.

SUNBURN

Grate a raw potato into a clean handkerchief. Fold the handkerchief into a square and apply it to the sunburned area for soothing and cleansing relief.

Alternatively, you can swab sunburned skin with some chilled white distilled vinegar. Do this every 15 minutes or so.

TINNITUS

Sometimes a ringing sound in the ear is caused by a build-up of wax in the ear. Have a look at the treatment for earache and try it out if you have tinnitus.

THRUSH

A thrush infection is alkaline so vinegar works against it. Put a cup of apple cider vinegar in your bath water and sit in it for a while so that the affected area is bathed. Make sure you don't get any in your eyes as it will sting.

WARTS

Okay, I'm not going to recommend rubbing raw meat on a wart before burying it in the garden, even if grandma did use the technique on me when I was a child. Instead, mix together a lotion made from apple cider vinegar and glycerine in equal measure. Apply it to the wart every day until it disappears.

SECTION 7

Beauty

My grandmother lived well into her nineties and managed to keep a youthful glow about her all her life. I'm hoping some of it was in the genes, but to listen to her talk, it was largely to do with the beauty regimes she followed throughout her life.

She didn't spend much money on beauty products, she couldn't afford it. Instead, she relied on the techniques which her own mother had told her about. They involved using many items that were readily available in the kitchen cupboard. I've collected them here, as well as adding a few extra that my research has thrown up.

SKIN

Freckles can be cute but if you're troubled by them you can use lemon juice to make them fade. Rub a little of the undiluted juice on them every day and within a few weeks you should begin to notice the difference.

Applying a good-quality mayonnaise to your skin every morning and night will help reduce the appearance of fine lines.

You can exfoliate by mixing a tablespoon of sea salt in a glass of hot water. Leave it to cool and then rub it gently over your upper lip to reduce fine vertical lines.

Get that sun-kissed look by moisturising your skin. If it is soft and smooth it is less likely to flake and peel upon exposure to the sun.

Give your face a hot, steam bath every few weeks to remove impurities. Just cover your head with a towel and put your face over a bowl filled with hot water.

If you suffer with greasy skin or acne then you could try splashing your face with water to which a couple of capfuls of apple cider vinegar have been added. Let your face dry naturally, without using a towel.

Milk of magnesia can be applied to spots to dry them out. More serious cases of acne can be treated using propolis, a resin collected by bees. It is available from friendly beekeepers or health food shops and it has an antibacterial effect. If you buy it in the shops you can get it in ointment form. Otherwise, warm and soften it in your hands before applying to acne.

Get rid of boils by increasing the blood flow to them. Apply a hot compress for several minutes, followed by a cold compress for one minute. If you repeat three times a day the boil will either come to a head or disappear altogether. You might want to try sprinkling cayenne pepper over the hot compress as this will stimulate the blood flow even further.

When you take a shower, turn off the hot water for 30 seconds before you get out. Cold water will increase the blood circulation and also the oxygen to your skin.

NATURAL FACE MASKS

Face masks work by removing the dead layer of outer skin, increasing blood flow to the surface and cleansing pores. Before choosing which one to use you need to find out about your skin type.

To do this, give your face a good cleansing before you go to bed. Next morning take a piece of toilet tissue that is just one layer thick. Press it to your face. If your skin leaves a few greasy marks behind then you have a greasy skin type. You will know if your skin is dry because it will feel a little taut after washing with soap and water. You may also have distinct areas of the face which are greasy and others that are normal or dry. You should treat these areas separately if you can. All the face masks listed can be left on for 20 minutes or so.

- For oily skin you can make a face mask by adding a teaspoon of lemon juice to a small tub of natural yoghurt.
- Another recipe that you can use for oily skin is honey with a

few drops of lemon juice added.

- Try using honey on its own for dry skin, but if you mix in some bran it will be even better. Just don't let anyone see you for 20 minutes until you've had a chance to let it do its work. Remove it with warm water.
- Mix up some egg yolk and evaporated milk for use on dry skin.
- Egg whites can be used as a make-do face mask. Beat them into a froth first and then allow to dry on the skin. If you have oily skin you should try adding a teaspoon of honey to the egg whites. Once the mask has dried you can wash it off with warm water.

HAIR

If your hairline, face, neck or hands become stained with hair dye you will need to find a friend who smokes. The ash from a cigarette will remove the stain if you rub it on with your fingertips.

Healthy hair requires a healthy scalp. Increase the blood flow to your scalp and strengthen your roots by massaging regularly. Knead it with your fingers.

After washing your hair, try massaging cold tea into it before rinsing. You will find your hair becomes shiny and will feel soft to the touch.

If your hair has become very dry you need to take a trip to your fridge. Wash your hair first and towel dry. Apply mayonnaise and leave it in the hair for up to an hour. Shampoo again and add a tablespoon of apple cider vinegar to the final rinse.

Change your shampoo regularly. If you don't then it will build up in your hair making it lank and lifeless. Alternatively, you can add a teaspoon of baking soda to the shampoo while you wash. Don't overdo this as repeated washing with baking soda may dry your hair out.

If you like to swim you will know that the chlorine in pools can damage hair, causing it to lose its natural shininess. It's a particular problem for those with red hair. You can protect against it to some extent by applying conditioner to your hair before swimming but short of wearing a cap there will always be some damage. You can, however, do something about it. Always rinse your hair in the shower after a swim. As you do so add a tablespoon of baking soda to half a cup of lemon juice and work it through your hair while it is still fizzing. This will help to counteract the effect of the chlorine.

HANDS, NAILS AND FEET

If your hands become chapped, try mixing lemon juice, rosewater and glycerine in equal parts before rubbing it in.

Get rid of unsightly nicotine stains on your fingers by giving up smoking. Only joking. Rub with lemon juice.

If your brittle fingernails are always breaking then try eating a square of jelly every now and again. Otherwise, bathe them in a solution of one part apple cider vinegar to eight parts water for ten minutes a couple of times a week.

Buff your nails regularly to strengthen them. Make sure you buff in one direction only.

Another way to add strength to nails is to soak them in a cup of water to which two teaspoons of salt have been added. Give them a good soak for two minutes once or twice a week.

Add baking soda to your washing-up water. It will soften your skin and help to clean the dishes.

If your ankles are thick and puffy it could be down to poor circulation. Try taking cayenne tea every day. This is made by dissolving half a teaspoon of cayenne pepper powder in a glass of warm water. It really does improve the blood flow. Have a look at the health section of this book for more information. You should avoid crossing your legs and whenever relaxing you should try and put your feet up.

Before you cut your toenails soften them up by bathing your feet in warm water with a couple of shakes of baking soda added. Not only will your nails be easier to cut but the water will help to soften the skin and deodorise your feet as well. Cut your toenails straight across and use an emery board to file down the corners.

EYES

Place a still-damp, cold tea bag over each eye while you lie down and relax for ten minutes. This will help tighten up any bags under the eyes. Splash the eyes with cold water when you've finished.

To promote the growth and health of eyelashes, brush them every day with almond oil using your eyebrow brush.

MAKE-UP

Leave your eyebrow pencil in the fridge for an hour before attempting to sharpen it. The wax 'lead' will harden and it will be easier to get the point you need.

You can use cold milk to remove make-up. Just soak a cotton wool bud in it.

You can make a great eye make-up remover yourself using sweet almond oil which is cheap and smells gorgeous as well. All you need to do is add two tablespoons of castor oil to six tablespoons of the almond oil. Use cotton wool to apply it. As an added bonus it will condition your eyelashes.

Oily skin holds scent for longer than dry skin. You can make your perfume last longer by applying a thin layer of Vaseline or another brand of petroleum jelly before spraying.

To prevent the lid of your nail varnish from sticking to the bottle, simply rub some petroleum jelly around the thread on the neck.

DENTAL HYGIENE

Polish your teeth by sprinkling dry salt on your toothpaste. Brushing regularly with baking soda, a mild abrasive, will also polish. Just dip your brush in it before adding the toothpaste. It will leave your teeth feeling as if you have just been polished by the dentist.

Try dipping your dental floss in baking soda before using. Its mildly abrasive qualities will keep the gaps between your teeth nice and sparkling white.

You can mix up your own toothpaste. Add three tablespoons of baking soda to a tablespoon of finely-ground salt. Mix together with a tablespoon of glycerine to thicken and a little boiled water. To make the whole thing more pleasant to the taste add a few drops of peppermint or spearmint essential oil or even food flavouring. If you want to add some fluoride protection then you can add a few drops of a mouthwash.

To remove stains and get your teeth nice and white mix half a teaspoon of lemon juice into a paste with a teaspoon of baking soda. Rub it over your teeth and leave for a few minutes before rinsing your mouth well and brushing. You should do this no more than once a week and NEVER use lemon juice on its own. Citric acid can actually damage the enamel on teeth if it is too strong or used too often.

If you wear dentures, you can get them sparkling white by placing them in a glass of full-strength white distilled vinegar for 15 to 30 minutes. Give them a good brushing afterwards. You can soak dentures overnight in a solution of water and baking soda. Two teaspoons in a glass should do the trick.

OTHER

A thin paste made with baking soda and water makes an excellent replacement for shaving foam. It has the added advantage of keeping your razor nice and clean.

You can pat baking soda under your arms for a cheap and effective deodorant. This is particularly useful for those who tend towards an allergic reaction when using other products.

Healing Juices

HEALTHY BENEFITS FOR ALL

Everyone knows that fresh fruits and vegetables are an essential part of a healthy diet.

They are packed with vitamins and minerals, they help us to maintain a healthy weight and they contain plenty of fibre to keep our digestive systems ticking along nicely.

It doesn't stop there. Many fruits and vegetables contain antioxidants which studies have shown to help resist cancer, and there is evidence they will also reduce the risk of heart attack and strokes when eaten in sufficient quantities.

Above all perhaps, they are delicious.

Doctors and nutritionists advise we take at least five portions of them a day. For many, however, this can seem a struggle. If you're one of those people then you should really consider investing in a juicer.

It is far easier to drink rather than eat our way to the target as we don't feel as full. Also, juicing breaks down the cells in fruit and vegetables which helps release their vitamins and minerals, making it easier for the body to absorb and use them.

It is also worth noting that cooking fruit and vegetables can destroy much of its goodness. As raw produce is used for juicing this is not a problem.

In other words, we get a greater benefit from drinking juices than we do from eating the corresponding fruits and vegetables.

THE TRADITIONAL HOUSEHOLD HANDBOOK

CHOOSING A JUICER

To juice fruit and vegetables you will need to invest in a juicer. There are hundreds on the market but here are a few pointers to help you select the best one for you.

In order to make sure your juicer doesn't end up stored at the back of a cupboard alongside the long-forgotten toasted sandwich maker and the soda stream, you need to select one that is easy to maintain. Make sure the one you choose has removable parts for washing and if you have a dishwasher then select one that is dishwasher safe.

Look for one with a wide mouth so that you can feed it bigger chunks of fruit and vegetables, thus saving chopping time.

Try to find one with non-slip rubber feet and if you are bothered by noise, a quiet one.

As always, it's best to get one on the recommendation of a friend or to try it out first. If you wait until the sales you will get a better juicer for your money.

SOME GENERAL HINTS AND TIPS WHEN JUICING

- Make sure you give fruit and vegetables a thorough wash with water before using.
- Remove any damaged portions before feeding fruit and vegetables into the juicer.
- Juice the stems and leaves because they contain goodness too. However, the leaves and stems of carrots are toxic so you will need to get rid of them.
- Do not juice the rind of grapefruits and oranges as they contain toxins.
- The pith from all citrus fruits, including oranges and grapefruits, is good for juicing as it contains plenty of vitamin C and bioflavonoids.
- You can stir any remaining pulp into your juice. It contains plenty of fibre.
- The goodness in juice is perishable so it is best to make your juice just before you are going to drink it. Just think about

how quickly a cut apple turns brown upon contact with oxygen and you will get the idea.

If you do want to store your juice then fill your container to the brim and cover with an air-tight lid. The container should be opaque to prevent light from destroying any of the goodness.

- Try and drink your juice at room temperature.
- The juice from some green vegetables can be somewhat of an acquired taste. To improve the flavour and make it palatable, try adding a few seedless grapes or some apple slices to the mix.
- Garnish the juice with salt, pepper, lemon juice, cinnamon, parsley, fennel or whatever else springs to mind. Just use your imagination to improve the look and taste of juices.
- You can add a few drops of essential oil to your juices. Fish oil is a valuable source of Omega 3 fatty acids as is flaxseed oil. Add cod liver oil for a boost in vitamins A and D. Evening primrose oil contains important Omega 6 fatty acids.
- Every now and again you can give your juicer a good clean by running a few drops of bleach through it. Wash thoroughly with water before you juice again.

AN A-Z OF AILMENTS AND THEIR JUICY TREATMENTS

Abdominal Pain

Try drinking the juice of citrus fruits and ginger.

Allergy

Beneficial juices include beetroot, carrot, celery, cucumber, nettle, parsley, pumpkin and spinach.

Anaemia

As Popeye knew, spinach has a high iron content so will help boost your red blood cells and combat anaemia. It is particularly beneficial for women whose need increases during menstruation.

Anxiety

Try adding fennel or peppermint to your drinks if you are anxious or suffer from anxiety attacks.

Aphrodisiac

Asparagus and ginger are said to boost the sex drive.

Appetite

Juniper berries are said to promote a healthy appetite. This explains why gin, made from juniper berries, is a common aperitif.

You can also use other appetite boosters, such as Brussels sprouts and dandelions.

Arthritis

Ginger. Danish researchers found patients who consumed ginger reported fewer symptoms, including pain, stiffness and swelling.

Celery mixed with citrus juice is said to relieve arthritis and rheumatism.

Studies over the years have shown cherries can treat the symptoms of arthritis.

Cucumber juice is good, as is apple, avocado, carrot, dandelion, fennel, garlic, nettle, juniper, strawberry and watermelon.

Asthma

Carrot, celery, cranberry, citrus fruits, watercress and grapefruit are all said to be beneficial.

Backache

Try strawberry or pomegranate juice for aches and pains in the back.

Biliousness

A juice made from the leaves and flowers of dandelions is a good remedy for biliousness.

Try drinking apple juice but remember to leave the peel on.

Additional juices to try include carrot, celery and spinach.

Bladder

For bladder problems, beetroot, cucumber, lemon, parsley and spinach are all said to be effective.

Blood Pressure

Beetroot juice is used in Romany medicine to reduce blood pressure.

Cucumber juice is good for high blood pressure.

Boils

Carrot, cucumber, lettuce, nettle and strawberry are all said to help prevent and be effective in treating boils.

Cancer

Cabbage, sprouts and broccoli are all rich in compounds which are said to reduce the risk of cancer. Tomato and ginger will help improve the flavour.

Catarrh

Try adding a clove or two of garlic to your juice to treat catarrh.

Cholesterol

Carrots have a high pectin content, so adding a couple to your juice may reduce cholesterol.

Garlic and onion juices have been found to reduce cholesterol. It is an excellent idea to take them following a fatty meal. The medical journal *The Lancet* said: "Both garlic and onion juices have now been found very significant in preventing the fat-induced increase in serum cholesterol and plasma fibrinogen."

Circulation

The juice of onions or raspberries is said to improve the flow of blood to the extremities.

Colds and Flu

Its hot, mustard-like properties mean adding a small amount of horseradish root to your juice will help clear sinuses. Be careful though, as it will be very hot. Try it with some lemon juice added. The vitamin C in the juice will boost your body's defences.

Take a cup of onion juice, add a cabbage leaf and simmer for five minutes. Add some honey to taste and drink as hot as possible. It should help relieve the symptoms of stuffy colds and flu.

Add a few peppermint leaves to your juice. It is good for unblocking the sinuses and relieving headaches associated with stuffiness.

Constipation

Try drinking the juice of a cucumber.

Cantaloupe has a lovely sweet, orange-coloured flesh and also has a laxative effect.

Radish juice is also an effective treatment for the symptoms of constipation.

Other juices that are helpful include apple, apricot, grape, lemon, pea, raspberry, strawberry and watercress.

Indeed, any fruit or vegetable rich in fibre will help keep your movements regular.

Coughing

Onion juice has been used to treat persistent coughs for centuries, and acts as an expectorant for when you are clogged up with phlegm.

Cystitis

Cranberry juice helps to fight this painful infection.

Depression

A boost of vitamin C from lemon will help to alleviate irritability and depression.

Detox

Apple is taken during detoxification as it reduces acidity in the body.

Fennel juice is effective in removing toxins from the body and is great for treating alcohol poisoning.

Diabetes

The intake of nettles has been shown to lower blood sugar. Just be careful when you are collecting them.

Digestive System

As well as improving the flavour of many juices, ginger is used to boost digestion and liver function. It is said to improve the production of gastric juices and reduce flatulence.

Cantaloupe is said to be effective in easing the symptoms of Crohn's disease which include a narrowing of the bowel and upset stomach.

Try nettle juice for the relief of diarrhoea.

Peppermint is an excellent leaf to add to your juice as it helps control diarrhoea and spasms as well as relieving indigestion.

Diuretic

Parsley juice is excellent for ridding the body of excess water.

Dizziness

Gooseberry juice is said to combat dizziness. If you find your head swims when you get out of your seat too fast then this could be the answer for you.

Earache

A few drops of warmed ginger juice in the ear will help reduce the pain.

Eyes

High in vitamin A, apricots can help with night-blindness and sties. They will also add lustre to your eyes.

Carrots, fennel and pumpkins can also be used to promote healthy eyes and good vision.

Flatulence

Take ginger to reduce flatulence.

Gout

A regular intake of nettle juice is said to relieve the symptoms of gout. Juniper berries will ease painful gout when juiced and drunk.

Adding strawberries to your juice will not only improve the flavour but will treat the symptoms of gout.

Halitosis

Parsley has been used for centuries to combat bad breath and is often taken following a meal rich in garlic.

In the Middle East the juice of pomegranates is used as a gargle for bad breath caused by yeast infection, rotting teeth and throat infections. Juice the pomegranates whole, including the skin. You will need to strain through a piece of muslin if you want to get rid of the seeds.

Hay Fever

Nettles have been used as a basis for the treatment of hay fever in many folk medicine remedies.

Try adding a local honey to your drink to combat hay fever. The pollen in local honey will be the same that makes your eyes stream as you go about your daily business, and taking it in honey form has an 'inoculating' effect.

Headache

Peppermint is good for relieving the pain of headaches. Take at the onset of an attack of a stress headache.

Heart

Hawthorn berries are rich in bioflavonoids and will strengthen blood-vessels and promote a healthy heart.

Other aids for a healthy heart include asparagus, carrot, celery, cherry, garlic, grape, lemon, nettle, onion and spinach.

Heartburn

If you get heartburn, then banana, dandelion leaf and root, fennel, peppermint and watermelon are all good cures.

Impotence

Ginger is said to improve blood flow and help with impotence.

Indigestion

Ginger-infused tea is used in India to treat indigestion.

Insomnia

Fennel juice, taken with a little honey, is said to be a cure for insomnia.

Lettuce is used as a cure for insomnia. As a general rule, the greener the leaves the greater the effect. Therefore, it is best to use a variety such as Romaine. Use all the leaves. The outer leaves, which are often discarded, contain the most nutrients.

Try adding a few rose petals when you juice your insomnia cure.

Irritable Bowel Syndrome

The medicinal benefits of drinking pea juice include the relief of irritable bowel syndrome. Peppermint is also helpful.

Joint Care

Fennel is used in folk medicine to ease pain, especially that of joints inflamed by rheumatism and arthritis.

Menstruation

The juice of raspberries can help relieve cramps. The high iron content in spinach can also help prevent anaemia which is sometimes associated with menstruation.

Migraine

Try taking a ginger drink with a little honey added.

Muscles

For aches, pains and twitches, try juicing ginger in your drink.

Nausea

Citrus fruits, ginger and apricot are all good for reducing nausea and preventing vomiting.

Nervous Tension

Celery juice is used as a nerve tonic to be drunk with meals or before going to bed. Lettuce is good also and it will help you sleep.

Neuralgia

Try adding some honey to nettle juice for treating neuralgia.

Rashes

Cucumber juice can be applied directly to a rash for relief.

Rheumatism

Asparagus was used in an old Romany cure for rheumatism.

Skin

Vitamins in carrots will help keep the skin healthy and free from spots, blackheads and whiteheads.

All fruits and vegetables containing vitamin C will help improve the skin. Lemons are particularly good. Lemons were used to combat scurvy and, during the 18th century, English ships were required by the Admiralty to carry lemon juice when embarking on overseas trips.

Try drinking a daily cup of parsley juice to improve the complexion.

A medium-sized tomato is said to provide half an adult's recommended daily intake of vitamin C and has excellent benefits for the skin. Leave the skin on the tomato when you juice.

Smoking

If you smoke it can deplete vitamin C reserves in the body. Lemon juice will help boost the supply of the vitamin.

Travel Sickness

Tests on new recruits to the US Navy found ginger root reduced the vomiting and nausea associated with rough weather and high seas.

Peppermint is excellent for treating motion sickness. Add a few leaves to your regular juice drink.

Varicose Veins

Strawberry juice is delicious, so is no problem at all to drink. It is said to relieve all inflammations of the blood-vessels, so is good for the treatment of varicose veins.

Warts

Juice made from the leaves and stems of dandelions should be rubbed into warts twice a day until they disappear.

Weight

If you take celery juice as part of a calorie-controlled diet it can promote weight loss.

Wrinkles

Fennel juice was used by Romany folk to smooth out wrinkles.

Index